PRIVATE GARDENS
OF
GEORGIA

PRIVATE GARDENS
OF
GEORGIA

POLLY McLEOD MATTOX *and* HELEN MATTOX BOST
Photographs by ERICA GEORGE DINES

Gibbs Smith, Publisher
TO ENRICH AND INSPIRE HUMANKIND
Salt Lake City | *Charleston* | *Santa Fe* | *Santa Barbara*

previous spread
'Cécile Brunner' roses entwine around the arch leading to the garden of Mr. and Mrs. Ted Plomgren.

this page
Foxgloves abound under the cedar fencing in the garden of Mr. and Mrs. Vern Davis.

First Edition
12 11 10 09 08   5 4 3 2

Text © 2008 Polly McLeod Mattox and Helen Mattox Bost
Photographs © 2008 Erica George Dines

Published by
Gibbs Smith, Publisher
P.O. Box 667
Layton, Utah 84041

Orders: 1.800.835.4993
www.gibbs-smith.com

Designed by Sarah Bolles
Printed and bound in China

Library of Congress Cataloging-in-Publication Data

Mattox, Polly McLeod.
 Private gardens of Georgia / Polly McLeod Mattox and Helen Mattox Bost ;
photographs by Erica George Dines. — 1st ed.
     p. cm.
 ISBN-13: 978-0-941711-98-2
 ISBN-10: 0-941711-98-6
 1. Gardens—Georgia. 2. Gardens—Georgia—Pictorial works. I. Bost,
Helen Mattox. II. Dines, Erica George. III. Title.
 SB466.U6M38 2008
 712'.609758—dc22
                         2007028432

To Kendrick Ware Mattox, Jr., and William Lewis Bost III

CONTENTS

Large boxwoods frame the white picket gate to the garden of Mr. and Mrs. Charles Miller,
while Confederate jasmine wraps around the arch above.

FOREWORD

Gardening is a lifestyle chosen by those who pursue its pleasure to be the fulfillment of one of the greatest of Southern traditions. The making of a garden serves an individual purpose, most importantly the need for us as humans to tackle that which is nature and manipulate her into a painterly setting. It is as important to have a sense of design as it is to validate why anyone would take on such an arduous task. By design I mean a conscious relationship between the house and garden, providing its maker with the opportunity for self-expression and, in the process, an individual paradise.

The extension of the house into the garden and making them integral provides the garden maker more room in which to indulge one's self in the rich pleasures of nature. More rooms to accessorize—rooms full of music made by birds and the sound of water, rooms where the sky is the ceiling and where clouds pass over, creating shadows, and where the wind blows ever so gently, changing the mood of the moment. The air is sweetened with the fragrance of flowers, which for us in Georgia is twelve months out of the year and has become the focus of making my own garden in Decatur, Georgia.

It is the heart of the garden that gives rise to the human need to share. That sharing is the opening of the gate to the outside world—"Come over and see the garden"—in the same way that each person in this book has filled its pages with their personal lives. I write some prose to fulfill my need to be a poet, and on July 2, 2007, I awakened to contemplate what is a garden the day before

I began to write the foreword for this book on private Georgia gardens for Polly Mattox and her daughter, Helen Bost. These are those thoughts that I share with you.

A garden and its making
is an intimate relationship
with nature.
Not unlike the human ethos,
which requires weeding,
refining an occasional
full-scale revamping.
This makes way for a new plant,
relationships and new memories.
None of the past need be forgotten;
they simply achieve
a more permanent place
in our memory,
never to be forgotten
but often revisited
in our dreams.

When Polly Mattox came to me with the idea of making a new book on the gardens of Georgia, I thought, what a lovely idea: a mother-daughter collaboration, embracing that southern tradition. I have worked with Mr. & Mrs. Mattox (Polly) for years in the making of their garden, and most recently with Helen Bost and the beginning stages of her garden. Their willingness to share their time in making this book, for all of us to continue to enjoy the opportunity to peer through the gate into these gardens, captures the spirit of true gardening, which is to share.

Ryan Gainey

In the garden of Ryan Gainey, a striking windmill palm is visible just above the bird feeder designed by Ryan and surrounded by *Hydrangea arborescens* 'Annabelle'.

ACKNOWLEDGMENTS

There are so many wonderful people to whom we are grateful for making this book possible. First of all, I have to thank my sister Margaret, whose idea it was. Secondly, our husbands: Ken, my husband—Helen's father—was a great help going over all of the text with us. Helen's husband, William, was wonderful to help out more than usual with their two girls, Heyward and Anne. William's mother, Ruthanna, is the best mother-in-law Helen could ask for. She kept Helen's children whenever she was needed. Many times, the little girls came along with us to the gardens.

Ryan Gainey, Hugh Dargan, Bill Smith, John Howard, Brooks Garcia, David Dempsey, Jim Gibbs, Alex Smith, Randy Korando, and Dan Cleveland were very helpful in showing us gardens they had designed. Alden Maier, Charlie Crisp, Mary Morrison, Jeanie Allen, and Kay Allen were all so wonderful to spend time showing us their areas of Georgia and giving us insight to other connections around the state. Michael Anderson and Maude Huff were a great help in Columbus. Everywhere we went the people were so gracious, inviting us into their lovely gardens. Staci Catron-Sullivan, the director of Cherokee Garden Club Library in Atlanta, and Jo Steele Phillips, the horticulturist at Hills and Dales Estate in LaGrange, helped us with our research to determine the proper way to punctuate plant names.

The most important thanks go to Pete Wyrick and Gibbs Smith for wanting to publish our book and making this all possible. For everyone, we are truly thankful.

- In the garden of Mr. and Mrs. Bill Jones III, soft lavender blooms of agapanthus draw the eye beyond the central parterre.

- In the garden of Ryan Gainey, golden boxwoods in terracotta pots designed by Ryan mark the entrance into the Borders Garden while tiles adorn the wall and *Salvia guaranitica* flourishes below.

INTRODUCTION

I have always loved beautiful gardens; large and small, it makes no difference. I cannot tell you how many books I have on gardens from around the world.

The genesis of this book was somewhat spontaneous. One day I was visiting my sister Margaret von Wersowetz at her home in Charleston, South Carolina. While I was reading one of her books on Charleston gardens, she suggested that I write a book about Georgia gardens. Well, it seemed like a fabulous thing to do.

When I got back to Georgia a few days later, I called my daughter, Helen, who is a marvelous writer, and said let's write a book about private gardens of Georgia. She thought this was a wonderful idea. While talking to my good friend and garden designer Ryan Gainey, I told him of our plan. He, too, thought it was an excellent idea and encouraged us to do it. That is how our great adventure began.

We contacted landscape architects who are active in Georgia and called friends from across the state. Everyone was enthusiastic about showing us gardens that they either designed or knew about in their area. There are many beautiful gardens in Georgia. It was extremely difficult selecting only thirty. Pete Wyrick, our editor, insisted that thirty would be as many as we could handle at once, and he was right. There was just not enough time to photograph and write about more and have the book published in a timely manner. Our thirtieth garden did not materialize

because of the extreme weather this spring. Georgia had an unusually warm March followed by freezing weather in the first part of April. Unfortunately, one garden simply did not recover in time.

Helen and I hope that you enjoy reading this book and that you are inspired in your own garden by the gardens featured here. We feel fortunate to have met the various garden owners and designers and to have learned the fascinating stories behind their creations. We had a marvelous time traveling the beautiful state of Georgia together with Erica Dines, our photographer and now friend. Writing this book with my daughter has been a rewarding endeavor and truly a labor of love.

—*Polly M. Mattox*

A gate leading into the author's garden.

A CITY GARDEN

THE GARDEN OF
JAMES MORTON

On the corner of two busy streets in Savannah lies the serene garden of James Morton shadowed by low boughs of live oaks dripping in Spanish moss. Morton bought the property in 1973 and converted the old home, originally built in 1856, back from apartments. He has an antiques store on the lower level and lives on the top two stories. Originally this was just "flat and dirt and nothing else," declares Morton. He has totally transformed his small space, designing three distinct and exceptional gardens.

The first garden, the Sunken Parterre Garden, is centered by a magnificent iron fountain set in a dense rectangular parterre consisting of three squares of boxwoods. Brick edging borders the dramatic, angular parterre and creates short terraces on each side, adding a real sense of depth to the garden. "I dug up the dirt and created terraces to make it appear longer than it is," says James. The first level is planted with alternating boxwoods and azaleas while the upper level is planted with tall evergreens. Japanese black

A gorgeous iron gate marks the entrance to the lush garden.

pines, which he dwarfed—"They'd be as tall as the roof otherwise."—flank either side of the garden entrance and add to the lavish green feel of the space.

A pair of grand stone finials atop low brick walls flanks the steps under a simple arch curtained in Confederate jasmine and leads to the Compass Garden. Here, rich boxwoods stand between four circles of topiary ilex fashioned with the letters N, S, E, and W for the compass points encircling the central ilex compass. Stunning bonsai are displayed around the periphery of the garden while a fantastic Italian oil jug marked with the Medici crest sits elevated behind the compass parterre. A vivid pair of potted lemon trees flanks the entrance to the quaint Sitting Garden, where splendid maples and azaleas set a calm stage in front of

a guesthouse whose iron balcony is wrapped with alluring, ancient wisteria. "We went through a stage where the wisteria was pulling down the iron rail," James says. "Now it is holding it up."

⠙ A beautiful iron fountain graces the middle of the central boxwood parterre in the Sunken Parterre Garden.

⠋ The iron fountain from the Sunken Parterre Garden stands on axis with the antique Italian jug in the Compass Garden just visible through the Confederate jasmine arch.

⠑ The Medici crest marks the front of this antique Italian oil jug in the Compass Garden.

⠛ A collection of bonsai encircles the periphery of the Compass Garden.

⠫ Holly, ferns and ivy surround a putti in the Sunken Parterre Garden.

⠻ N, S, E, and W are clipped in the ilex and boxwood parterre of the Compass Garden.

BLACK BANKS

THE GARDEN OF
MR. AND MRS. BILL JONES III

Black Banks is a gorgeous tract of land on St. Simons Island. It lies
on the edge of the Black Banks River and the extensive marshes that separate
St. Simons Island from Sea Island. Originally owned by the Gould family
from the early nineteenth century until well after the Civil War, it was one
of the many Sea Island cotton plantations that thrived on this land years
ago. The beautiful American Federal–style home that stands here today was
built in the late 1930s by owners who replaced the original three-story, cottage-
style tabby that served as the main house of the plantation.

The entry to Black Banks is marked by a beautiful wrought-iron gate
between brick columns extending from a simple brick wall, all bathed in dense
fig vine. The home, hidden by cascades of Spanish moss, sits far back to the
right across a lush field of grass. The property abounds with a variety of ferns,
azaleas, camellias, hydrangeas, palms, and massive live oaks. It is the enchanting
live oaks that really define this lowcountry area of Georgia. They impart a feel
of majestic beauty and history, and they evoke a sense of romance.

Sally and Bill Jones III purchased this magnificent property in 2002.
Bill is the chairman and CEO of Sea Island Company, which owns the
famed Cloister resort on Sea Island directly across the river. Bill's grandfather,

Crepe myrtles and agapanthus frame the view out
to the Black Banks River and the marsh beyond.

A. W. Jones, Sr., and Jones's older cousin, Howard Coffin, opened the Cloister in 1928. Coffin first purchased Sapelo Island before buying property on St. Simons, and then ultimately purchased Long Island, which he renamed Sea Island. They envisioned a fabulous beach resort and cottage community and together created what is now one of the most exclusive resorts in the country. Coffin turned the company over to A. W. Jones, Sr., whose son then ran the company, before his own son, Bill III, became president in 1992.

The gardens of Black Banks are simple; the setting is breathtaking and serves as a backdrop to the gardens, which blend in harmoniously with the marshlands. When Bill and Sally moved in, they had much of the scrub brush by the edge of the marsh cleared so as to take full advantage of the captivating view. They added about fifty or sixty exquisite old camellias throughout the property, and they planted more cedars, magnolias, azaleas, and hydrangeas. Increasing the beauty of the spot are old pots, antique urns, and olive jars that are kept planted year-round with vibrant displays of color. Meandering brick paths wind about past citrus trees, including massive orange, grapefruit, and lemon trees.

A magnificent live oak, dressed with Spanish moss, graces the front of the old home.

One of the many camellias on the property provides a contrast to the soft gray of the Spanish moss.

A pretty brick path meanders through the garden.

A variety of fabulous azaleas abound at Black Banks in the spring.

A beautiful lime tree stands at the center of the charming perennial garden.

The pool is situated beside the tidal Black Banks River.

At the back of the house is a parterre set directly on axis with the sweeping tabby steps. The densely green parterre is made up of boxwoods, sasanquas, podocarpus, dwarf yaupon holly, dwarf Indian hawthorn, and mondo. It is centered by a large iron jardinière planted with a rhapis palm surrounded with ivy spilling over the edge. A delicate and low stucco shell fountain anchors each side of the brick path that encircles the parterre; flowers and palms create the borders beyond. To the right, the charming "Tee-Hee" house graces the branches of a huge, bent live oak while a lovely secret garden is tucked away on the front left of the house. Separated by a white picket fence with vine-swathed arches marking the entrances, this garden serves as the cutting garden for the grand house. A lime tree stands in the center, while boxwood parterres on either side create an exquisite formal garden planted with herbs, roses, and annuals. Everything seems to thrive in this warm, lush climate.

The central parterre is made up of boxwoods, dwarf yaupon holly, sasanquas, podocarpus, dwarf Indian hawthorn, and mondo—all encircling a potted rhapis palm.

One of a pair of low stucco shell fountains accents the side of the central parterre.

The graceful boughs of this ancient live oak laden with Spanish moss stretch across the lawn to a mass of azaleas.

These live oaks create the perfect spot for a hammock.

The charming "Tee-Hee" house is nestled in one of the old live oaks.

A COASTAL GARDEN

THE GARDEN OF
MR. AND MRS. ROBERT BRUBAKER

Carol and Robert Brubaker live in a splendid Italianate home in the lush environment of St. Simons Island, where a Mediterranean feel seems to emanate and envelop the visitor. They have lived in this home since 1995 and have worked on their garden in stages, expanding slowly over time to create an impeccable series of formal gardens, all designed by Carol. Before beginning, the Brubakers traveled to Europe, where Carol found inspiration in the grand gardens at Sissinghurst Castle and other sites. They have a lot of acreage here, having taken advantage of a former vacant lot beside them.

Everything is perfectly proportioned and flows effortlessly through the varied gardens. Jasmine abounds on the trunks of tall trees while lime trees add to the sweet smell. "I love fragrance; fragrance is really important to me in the garden," says Carol. The façade of the home is warmed by a large grouping of massive azaleas and boxwoods. Tall Italian cypresses along with hybrid teas and exquisite antique roses complement the architecture.

The first garden, entered from the left side of the home, is the Rose Garden. A beautifully sculpted hedge accented by four tall, clipped Italian

Wisteria drapes over the massive doors leading into the Rose Garden, where asparagus fern masses over the pond and agapanthus begins to bloom.

cypresses frames a lush pond where asparagus ferns and agapanthus reign. Vibrant vitex trees and lime trees frame the steps leading up to the house and a variety of roses fill the borders. From here, a lustrous allée known as the White Garden beckons. Here glorious ginger lilies, gardenias, and quince abound under the gracious limbs of five pairs of white crepe myrtles. In the French Garden a beautiful lawn opens between borders of yaupon holly parterres, which turn a stunning red in the winter and are abloom with luscious roses through the spring and summer. Pear trees lend height and volume at each corner while magnificent urns proudly mark the four corners of the lawn. A pair of striking cherry laurel obelisks stands on the far side leading to the Italian Garden. The Japanese Garden can be accessed from the far corner.

Chinese temple doors the Brubakers found in Hawaii mark the entry to the extensive Japanese Garden where a beautiful stream meanders through lovely, wispy river birches and willows. They began this garden in 2000, though it seems as established

The beautifully sculpted hedge of the Rose Garden is accented by tall, clipped Italian cypresses.

'New Dawn' roses cover the arch leading out of the Rose Garden.

Magnificent doors lead from the Rose Garden into the White Garden.

White dianthus and white impatiens border the narrow lawn under the white crepe myrtle allée in the White Garden.

as the other gardens. "Everything here grows so quickly; it's hot, it's humid; everything loves it here," states Carol. Beautiful 'Bloodgood' maples and cherry trees fill the sky with their enchanting limbs, the former blazing brilliant red in the fall and the latter adding delicate pink blooms to the mix in the spring. A quaint bridge layered in wisteria arches over the stream, where an alluring display of water lilies takes hold among the pretty koi splashing about. Another set of grand Chinese temple doors leads you into the next garden, the Italian Garden. The beautifully mottled trunks and tremendous leaves of four grand London plane trees command attention. A simple fountain stands against the far wall and is framed by a hedge of espaliered pears. There are large pots of 'Meyer' lemons as well as kumquats.

Wisteria and fig vine engulf this pretty bridge in the Japanese Garden.

Beautiful topiary roses stand in the centers of the yaupon holly parterres on each side of the iron gate.

London plane trees give height to the Italian Garden.

Urns stand at the corners of the lawn in the French Garden.

A lovely statue anchors one end of the White Garden.

Yaupon holly parterres edge the French Garden, in addition to the urns at the corners of the lawn.

Old Chinese temple doors mark the entrance to the Japanese Garden.

IRIS COURT

THE GARDEN OF
CHARLES CRISP

Iris Court is a magnificent Greek Revival home originally built in 1853 in Albany and moved to Moultrie in 1961 by Charles O. Smith, Jr., who was married to the famous horticulturist Dean Day Smith. Situated on twenty acres of South Georgia land, this home and property have a mystical feel about them. Charlie Crisp moved here in 2004 from nearby Americus and has many ties with Moultrie, which was named by his great-grandfather. Charlie had been to parties here; he knew Dean Smith, and he knew the splendid house and grounds as well.

The house is marked on Tallokas Road by stately stucco walls and an open iron gate with tall conical hollies following a curved holly hedge. Iris Court is barely glimpsed through the long allée of live oaks whose low boughs are festooned with Spanish moss. As you head down the long dirt-and-pebble drive, azaleas and dogwoods flourish in the woods to each side while plantings of ferns and ginger lilies meet you closer to the path. A circular drive signals the end, where a set of five splendid crepe myrtles flanks each side and boxwoods border the timeless home.

Spanish moss drapes the view of Spring standing
elegantly among a mass of azaleas and magnolias.

Charlie hired Jim Gibbs to help with the landscape design. Enormous camellias are scattered throughout the property, along with pretty sago palms. Everything here seems to be on a grand scale. To the right of the house stands an alluring statue that Charlie added among magnolias, camellias, azaleas, and 'Dean Day' sasanquas, creating a loose garden. To the left of the house, asiatic jasmine grounds additional palms among ginger lilies, daylilies, and more magnolias. A hedge of thickly planted, voluminous azaleas leads to the back of the house. Set directly on axis with the rear façade, four rectangular boxwood parterres, each planted with two tall crepe myrtles, define the only formal garden of the property. Continuing the live oak allée of the front, fifteen pairs of majestic magnolias create a long allée behind Iris Court so that from all angles the view is simply stunning.

Stucco walls bathed in fig vine along with a pretty iron gate mark the entrance to Iris Court.

A lovely statue stands at the center of the boxwood parterre.

The Greek Revival home was built in 1853.

Small putti show the height of these crepe myrtles adorning the circular drive in front of the house.

Tall crepe myrtles and a single urn filled with seasonal plantings define the simple boxwood parterre behind the home.

A SOUTHERN GARDEN

THE GARDEN OF
MR. AND MRS. VICTOR BEADLES

Victor and Deryl Beadles live in a pretty 1965 Frank McCall–
designed home set on a classic South Georgia property in Moultrie.
The Beadles had this home built and began working on the garden
from day one. A fabulous grouping of expansive dogwoods, tall pines,
and lush azaleas frame the front drive. A manicured lawn stretches out
in the filtered shadows of scattered pines to the fig vine–covered
home where pretty boxwoods line the front and asiatic jasmine forms
the base.

The backyard is lined in a flat brick border that curves along
the contours of the grass under a hedge of immense pink and white
azaleas. A lattice swing sits to the right with tall crepe myrtles
lending height all along the back. A pretty bronze fountain the Beadles
found in France is planted with a mass of daffodils in a niche of
white azaleas. A lion's head fountain, another bronze from France,
is mounted to a brick wall bathed in fig vine. "I am a yard person,"
states Deryl, and she keeps this property in perfect condition.
Everything is as it is supposed to be; rarely will you find even a
pinecone out of place.

Sunlight filters through the dogwoods onto the azaleas below in this classic Southern garden.

A charming lead statue is nestled among the boxwoods by a maidenhair fern.

A bronze fountain from L'Isle-sur-la-Sorgue, France, is nestled in a niche of white azaleas.

A bronze lion's head fountain from L'Isle-sur-la-Sorgue, France, adorns this fig vine–covered wall.

A small eighteenth-century Italian putti highlights the corner of the pool house along with a potted windmill palm and maidenhair fern.

Magnificent dogwoods and azaleas frame either side of the driveway.

An urn planted with a beautiful sago palm marks the steps to the pool.

A GARDEN FOR ENTERTAINING

THE GARDEN OF
DR. AND MRS. LOGAN NALLEY, JR.

This lovely plantation-style home in Augusta was built between 1805 and 1810. When Logan and Dale Nalley bought the house, which is on the National Register, twenty years ago, they made several changes with the help of architect Al Cheatham. Two wings had already been added to the four-room home in the 1860s, and the once-separate kitchen had been attached to the back of the house and used as a laundry room. The Nalleys detached the old kitchen laundry room and made it a separate building once again. The configuration of the backyard is defined by several of these outbuildings: the old kitchen previously mentioned; a guest cottage to which they made some minor renovations; a greenhouse; and two playhouses.

About six years ago, landscape architect Bill Smith was recommended to them by Al Cheatham. Smith organized the space and created the compositions; with his help this refined garden has developed. "We wanted to separate the different areas," explains Smith. "It was all kind of the same level, a cross slope.

Spikes of 'Foxy' foxgloves stand out among the 'Liberty' snapdragons and pink and white dianthus in the spring border garden by the greenhouse.

We have a lot of architecture back here, so we separated the outbuildings from the main view and created their own gardens." The front of the house has its own garden. "In an old house like this, it is appropriate to have flowers in front," says Smith.

A large back patio with wide steps covered in fig vine echoing those in front is a connection between the house and garden. It is shaded by a pergola covered with dense jasmine and moon vine. A long allée of crepe myrtles edged with a boxwood border leads to a beautiful greenhouse designed by Al Cheatham in the midst of an abundance of flowers. Between the brick edging and white zinnias lies a carpet of grass that is capped by an elegant quatrefoil lawn with a koi pond in the center repeating the same motif. This is all directly on axis with the greenhouse and the back stairs and comprises the main garden, where the trickle of the fountain radiates a quiet serenity throughout the property.

The brick-bordered quatrefoil is backed with beds on either side of the greenhouse. These beds, like those in front of the house, have perennial backbones

A grapevine and 'New Dawn' roses envelop the light post at the front gate.

A pair of rose topiaries captures the eye among the spring annuals and perennials.

'New Dawn' roses adorn the light post by this sitting area.

A great view of the standard crepe myrtle allée and lawn leading to the greenhouse and koi pond is visible from the back patio.

Narrow-leaf zinnia highlights this boxwood hedge under the end of the 'Natchez' crepe myrtle allée by the guest cottage.

with annuals added twice a year. In the fall, white violas replace the zinnias in the crepe borders. In the spring, tulips, foxgloves, and snapdragons dominate the quatrefoil border. Then in summer, giant spikes of pink and white cleome take over, along with tall Oriental lily, and enormous swamp sunflowers. The abundance of soft flowers spilling over the borders relaxes the strict design of the garden. Dale also has a perfect little herb garden since she loves to garden, to cook, and entertain. It is laid out very cleverly along the back right side of the house, close to the kitchen. An old bee skep marks the center and gives the charming garden height while a box hedge defines the front. The sides are distinguished with terracotta baskets Bill had made. This small parterre garden is grounded with large basil plants and hardy rosemary. Aromatic herbs with delicate forms weave through and unite the space.

○○ ○ Spikes of white cleome stand out in the summer border
        garden by the greenhouse.

○○ ○ The millstone at the entrance of the greenhouse is centered
●   with ajuga and circled with dichondra.

○● ○ Inside the greenhouse.

○○ ● An old bee skep surrounded by lettuce centers this herb
        garden. Flowering chives and terracotta baskets planted
        with rosemary topiaries anchor the ends.

○○ ○ A pretty pair of red maples separates the pool garden
   ●   from the back garden.

JARDINS DES COEURS

THE GARDEN OF
MR. AND MRS. CHARLES MILLER

In 1985, Irene and Charles Miller built this great house in Milledgeville on five acres of fabulous old pastureland. This was part of famed Southern writer Flannery O'Connor's farm. The Miller's piece was part of the cow pasture, so there was not a single hardwood on the property. They had to establish their land before they began work on the garden itself.

In 1994, they hired landscape architect Ryan Gainey to develop a grand plan that has evolved since then into the magnificent garden of "organized disorder" that exudes such splendor today. "My garden in my mind is more of a nature thing," reveals Irene. The Millers planted an allée of stunning 'Bradford' pears up the drive culminating in a handsome motor court, which is enclosed with perennial beds on either side of the home. Massive 'Tardiva' hydrangeas flank the front door while a pair of viburnums marks the end of each hedge. The hedges curve out as a boundary to the dense beds beyond. From the rear, one enters the voluminous garden, walking out first onto a splendid terrace sheltered by a pergola

One of a pair of beautiful Chinese fringe trees can be seen just beyond the stone fountain, which is surrounded by large pots of rosemary.

'GARDENS OF THE HEART'

○ ○ A magnificent allée of 'Bradford' pears lines the drive.

○ ○ One of a pair of stone posts and stunning Japanese snowball viburnums that mark the beginning of the drive.

○ ● The pair of stone doorways leading to the Cedar Garden centers the large, terracotta strawberry pot overflowing with petunias in the middle of the side boxwood parterre.

○ ○ A boxwood hedge frames a fountain that sits between the pair of steps leading to the terrace.

where a plethora of potted lemon and lime trees fill the air with a glorious scent. The second terrace, with its refined fountain, is visible from here while the spacious garden is glimpsed just beyond.

A stone path to the right leads past a diamond boxwood parterre planted with the soft forms of Mexican sage and salvia, whose vivid colors captivate the eye. From here a pair of stone doorways marks the entrance into the

Cedar Garden, where a long, verdant lawn is totally enveloped by soaring cedars on all sides, creating an exquisite Italian hedge. Descending the central steps from the terrace into the lush display below, a boxwood hedge defines the edge of the long lawn while a pair of immense hollies lends height and volume to each side. Viburnums frame the summerhouse, whose form is blurred by a mass of cascading 'Lady Banks' roses. A delightful koi pond centered in front adds to the serenity of the spot. Graceful steps in the middle right hedge lead to a lovely circular garden while an arbor path swathed in fiveleaf akebia and evergreen clematis stands on axis across the lawn. The pool lies ahead in a walled garden where flowers shower down the stucco walls.

A mass of 'Lady Banks' roses engulfs the summerhouse at the end of the long lawn.

A striking 'Athena' elm reigns over the steps leading from the main lawn.

A close-up of the summerhouse shows the Japanese snowball viburnum and the cascades of the 'Lady Banks' rose.

Boxwoods enhance the wall and steps leading from the main lawn to the circular garden.

BANKSHAVEN

THE GARDEN OF
WILLIAM BANKS

Up a long, winding drive in Newnan, through the thick woods of this extraordinary property, sits "Bankshaven," the majestic, Federal home of William Banks. Originally designed and built in the 1820s by Daniel Pratt, the home was moved with the help of architect Robert L. Raley from the small town of Haddock near Milledgeville, Georgia. At the end of the drive, a cluster of oaks, protected below by a massive hedge of tea olives, stands to the left while a clearing in their midst sets off statues of the four seasons, which are set on axis with the back façade of the grand home. This is where William grew up, though in a different house. His parents bought the land, which includes the beautiful Pearl Spring Lake, in the twenties and built a Tudor-style home here. "Father cleared all of the woods on this side of Pearl Spring Lake; he wanted the house on the rise looking down on the lake," says Banks. He razed the old home and moved the current building, which sits in the same spot overlooking the lake. Entering the home through the rear, the central hall opens onto a set of double doors highlighted by a glorious fanlight. A loose planting of woods frames either side of the long vista down to the lake where Canada geese, peacocks, and swans move about.

William's mother began laying the gardens in 1929 with the help of famed landscape designer William C. Pauley, who worked on them from the 1930s through the 1960s.

The front double doors and their glorious fanlight
open onto the glittering lake beyond the lawn.

William inherited the property around 1970 and has done much to enhance the remaining 200 acres. "Gardens change so, but this is really the only private garden that is still essentially Pauley's design," he explains. The first garden entered is on the right of the house past exquisite magnolias and grand old English boxwoods. A pair of urns marks the stone steps down onto a lawn lined with a double-height row of boxwoods and culminating in a dazzling, three-tiered fountain. This Italian fountain, carved in the 1840s of gorgeous Carrara marble, is encircled by large boxwoods, making the height of the impressive fountain a necessity for the correct scale. To the left, a small garden bordered with azaleas and hydrangeas is entered through an iron arch swathed in flowering vines. Here, another beautiful Italian statue from the 1840s is highlighted. This is the next project; Banks uncovered the remains of one of Pauley's old designs and is working

to re-create an extension of this side garden.

On axis, to the right of the fountain, more immense boxwoods lead to a pool that is bordered on either side by a dense 'Fosteri' holly hedge. The far end is shaded by a whimsical tented pavilion, which is actually painted concrete. On either side of the pool, in the midst of the hedges, pairs of carved lava finials mark the entrances to more

The 1820s Federal home fronts the lake.

Small cherubs representing the four seasons are framed by the trunk of a white oak and the pale blooms of 'Pink Pearl' azaleas.

An iron table and chairs sit out on the lawn of the grand home.

One of a pair of eighteenth-century French terracotta lions, signed and dated, marks the steps down to the lake.

A brick path leads through the exquisite Boxwood Garden to the lattice gazebo framed by soft blooms of yoshino cherry trees and white dogwoods.

A beautiful Styrax tree frames this 1840s Italian statue that stands among a mass of azaleas.

gardens beyond. To the left is the magnificent Boxwood Garden composed of a maze of boxwoods that are more than one hundred years old. William's father moved them from a maze in Cousins, Georgia; the head gardener numbered them before transferring them and re-created the maze exactly as it had been. An elegant white lattice gazebo designed by architect Raley sits up to the left overlooking the boxwoods while four stunning yoshino cherry trees emphasize each corner and four white dogwoods fill the interior with their delicate boughs.

From here, a path leads out to the formal garden where brick paths with raised diamond brick edging lead through the profusion of planned beds. The first outer beds are filled with tulips, Dutch irises, and sweet williams in the spring, then zinnias and marigolds in the summer, and finally chrysanthemums in the fall. The center beds overflow with 'Betty Prior' roses that group around a single large bed of Knockout roses, which William exclaims is a "wonderful

Brick paths lead through the formal garden where beds of foxgloves, pansies, Dutch irises, and daisies border the central beds of peonies and roses.

A tented pavilion, which is actually painted concrete, stands at the far end of the pool.

A beautiful 1840s Italian fountain carved of Carrara marble is encircled by large boxwoods at the end of this lush lawn bordered by more of the old boxwoods.

rose because the foliage is so good, and it blooms all summer and it is fragrant as well." The last five beds are stunning peony beds that his mother first planted in the thirties. The farthest section is dominated by an armillary sphere in the midst of more seasonal beds. A low brick wall festooned with ivy surrounds this entire garden, while pairs of stone fruit baskets mark the entrances.

- Mazus and creeping jenny soften the stones surrounding this fabulous fountain encircled by English boxwoods. The puttino with dolphin is a copy of a famous Verrocchio statue in Florence, Italy. This copy is one of three original casts taken from the statue when it was being cleaned.

- Foxgloves, Dutch irises, sweet williams, and daisies create a stunning border in the formal garden.

- The lattice gazebo of the Boxwood Garden is framed by an arch in the hedge dividing it from the formal garden where spectacular beds of peonies, 'Betty Prior' roses, and Knockout roses create a sea of color.

THE AUTHOR'S GARDEN

THE GARDEN OF
MR. AND MRS. KENDRICK MATTOX, JR.

It is hard to know how to begin or where to start writing about this exquisite garden in LaGrange. Polly and Ken Mattox moved here in 1976. The home is a beautiful Ivey and Crook design built in 1938. It sits gracefully atop a gentle hill on a beautiful corner. One of the first things Polly and Ken did was to plant the four magnolias that now dominate the left side of the front lawn, lending privacy from the side street. They have recently planted two more on the right. Fabulous old cedars flourish on the property, in front and back, and add elegance and a touch of aura to the spot. Originally the backyard was a tall hill that terraced out naturally before rising again to the woods, with a lawn stretching in between two large rock gardens. A smaller rock garden on the left of the second rise was converted into a rose garden that Polly faithfully attends today. "I had always wanted a rose garden because my grandmother had a beautiful rose garden and kept cut roses in the house all summer," as does Polly. Her favorite rose is 'Tiffany' rose, while her grandmother's favorite was 'Queen Elizabeth'. 'Chicago Peace', 'Garden Party', and 'Peace' are some of the others that thrive among them.

Two additions have been made to the home, the last one completed in 2004. The first addition was designed by architect Randy Zaic in 1991. That is when the garden really began to take shape. There had been a nice side garden, but they really wanted a walled garden and a pool. Polly called upon Ryan Gainey to help with the landscaping. She was familiar with his gardens and was a regular in his old shop, The Potted Plant. Ryan convinced them to put the pool in the small side yard instead of on the long back terrace, and that dictated everything.

White impatiens line the stone steps up to a secret garden while oakleaf hydrangeas spill over the gracefully curved wrought-iron railing.

This side yard became the walled garden for which Polly had longed. It is centered by a beautiful arbor with shell stucco columns in front and a tall stucco wall behind, which defines the far side of the garden. Stretching across the space, thick locust wood beams drip in 'Lady Banks' roses in the spring, trumpet vine in the summer, and 'Mermaid' roses in both seasons. The Mattoxes often entertain under the arbor where a marble table is topped by a divine shell mirror. This is truly a magical spot steeped with the warmth of dense foliage and glorious flowers, surrounded by

nature. The elegant columns of the arbor sit at the edge of the black-bottom pool, framing the graceful steps that lead into the water. Tennessee crab orchard coping defines the elegant shape of the pool while stone balls mark each corner and, with a switch, turn the pool into a fountain as they delicately spout water that meets in the center.

The west wall of this garden is formed by a stacked wall of crab orchard stone. Above this is a rock garden containing an enchanting display of oak-leaf hydrangeas, 'Annabelle' hydrangeas, and masses of 'Miss Huff' lantana. The east wall is stucco with espaliered sasanquas and climbing roses on either side of a central niche that houses an alluring statue of Summer framed by a pair of windmill palms and bathed with 'Annabelle' hydrangeas and ferns. The perimeter is planted with lush grass bordered by Asiatic jasmine. On the far side, further defining the edges of the arbor, stands a pair of tall 'Natchez' crepe myrtles. A pair of small standard 'Alba' wisteria trees marks either side of the pool with heavy white blooms hanging over a low hedge of boxwoods encircling white impatiens below. An elegant wrought-iron railing leads up the winding stone steps to a secret garden, presenting a stunning view over the rock garden to the walled garden below. A scattered stone floor of the same stone carpeted with moss sets the stage for an old stone table and benches enclosed by massive boxwoods on one side and azaleas on the other. From here, a path leads to the upper rose garden.

'Rêve d'Or' roses cascade over the stucco wall of the motor court where foxgloves and verbascums bloom in the spring behind the manicured boxwood hedges.

A Chinese snowball viburnum can be seen from the front of the Ivey and Crook home.

A pair of lush windmill palms frames this pretty statue of Summer surrounded by ferns and 'Annabelle' hydrangeas beyond the dark pool.

At the base of these steps is the new patio created by the final addition, which was designed by architect Marc Mosley with Ryan Gainey and the Mattoxes. As the home and gardens have evolved, Gainey has provided the vision and made sure the house and gardens flow one into the other. Nowhere is this clearer than this little patio situated between the French doors of the main body of the house and the French doors of the latest addition. It simply feels green amid all the pretty pots planted with seasonal flowers as well as camellias and various shapes of boxwoods. One of the best touches of this garden is the plethora of planters: some terracotta, some stone, others iron; urns; and an olive oil jar.

The other new space formed by the addition is a motor court. A small arbor was built along the addition, which was made possible by a large stucco retaining wall cut into the old bank. This arbor is entwined with jasmine, 'Amethyst Falls' wisteria, and 'Etoile Violet' clematis. A delightful bench creates a restful spot between a pair of old

○ ○ 'Tiffany' roses stand in the foreground of
● ○○ the rose garden.

○ ○ A gracefully curved wrought-iron railing
● ○○ leads down the stone steps through
white impatiens, oakleaf hydrangeas,
and 'Sister Teresa' hydrangeas onto
the side terrace.

○ ● A fabulous pair of standard 'Alba' wiste-
○ ○○ rias flank the arbor, whose roof is
drenched in 'Mermaid' roses, 'Lady Banks'
roses, and trumpet vine. Sprays of water
cross the dark pool in front of the arbor.

○ ○ 'Alba' wisteria creates a spectacular
○ ●○ sight in the spring.

○ ○ A magnificent shell mirror and pink
○ ○● marble table complete this perfect spot
under the arbor.

'Amethyst Falls' wisteria and 'Etoile Violet' clematis climb the columns of the side arbor while 'Iceberg' roses bloom below.

'Iceberg' roses bloom behind the boxwood hedge while violet roses climb the wall by the steps to the back lawn.

'Miss Huff' lantana spills over the stacked stone wall in the summer.

A pretty stone table and benches stand at the center of a secret garden that is enclosed by boxwoods on one side and 'Mrs. G. G. Gerbing' azaleas on the other.

cherub statues that were Polly's grandmother's. A low boxwood hedge encloses three sides of the motor court and a splendid cryptomeria defines the left side. Giant spikes of foxgloves and verbascums stand out among the forget-me-nots in the spring while 'Iceberg' roses, 'Annabelle' hydrangeas, and 'Limelight' hydrangeas overflow behind the hedge in the summer and 'Ryan Gainey' yellow mums and 'Rachel Jackson' asters continue their bloom through the fall. Climbing hydrangeas grow on the tall stucco walls to meet the 'Rêve d'Or' roses, which cascade down from the old lawn above. Rocking chairs and other seating complete the spot, which is ideal for grandchildren and their tricycles. On the far side of the motor court, the matching wrought-iron railing leads beside the only part of the original rock garden kept totally intact. It is now filled with azaleas, 'Tardiva' hydrangeas, and 'Nikko Blue' hydrangeas while a vitex dominates the lower corner and three gracious dawn redwoods define the left side.

A COURTYARD GARDEN

THE GARDEN OF
BETTY MATTOX

This 1849 Greek Revival home in LaGrange was relocated from its original site in Grantville. The late Kendrick Mattox and his wife, Betty, had it moved, board by board, in 1967, to its current location, high up on a beautiful wooded hill. When they bought the lot in LaGrange, it was steeply sloped and had to be terraced, with a large plot dug down and out for the house.

There are three brick retaining walls on the property. The first retaining wall forms a level spot for the home. The chimney bricks from the original house were sand bricks and couldn't be reused in the chimney; instead, these bricks were used to build the retaining wall. Covered in fig vine, it stands behind a boxwood garden, which encircles a tall and stately iron fountain marking the center of the front lawn. Cherry trees stand at each front corner while 'Tardiva' hydrangeas flourish within. This central garden serves almost as an ornament enhancing the elegant façade of the home along with the softening touches of boxwoods that line the perimeter of the house. Some of these massive boxwoods are over one hundred years old; many were moved from their former home in Hogansville.

Magnolias frame the Greek Revival home built in 1849.

As you pull up the paved gravel drive, a pair of stone urns atop brick pillars marks the entry to the motor court. The second retaining wall, covered in dense sasanquas, begins along the right side and is planted with enormous camellias and rhododendrons before it cuts to the left and extends along the back of the property. The main courtyard garden is on this level, just beyond the breezeway. The courtyard is a small walled garden consisting of a low, circular hedge of boxwoods surrounding a central brick patio with a smaller, refined iron fountain marking the center, all within a larger grass square. Graceful iron seating completes the inner circle while annuals enhance the outer ring and planted urns stand at each crossing of the herringbone brick path that leads to the gardens beyond. "This is really an annual garden," notes Betty. It is planted two times a year with tulips, azaleas, and plumbago in the spring and lantana, hydrangeas, and pintas taking over in the summer, all buzzing with bumblebees and butterflies.

Palm trees stand in each far corner of the courtyard with more annuals below, pansies, and then impatiens. Beyond the low walls of the courtyard,

an elegant white gazebo dominates. A pair of lead peacocks rests on top of the courtyard wall and marks the path to this lovely gazebo designed by Randy Zaic in the late 1980s. Stepping-stones lead to the left and right through thick hydrangeas. The brick path continues straight ahead to the steps of the gazebo, which are flanked by a pair of putti balanced upon stone capitals with large boxwoods on either side.

To the right of the courtyard, on axis with the fountain and just outside the courtyard wall, is a beautiful statue of Harvest. She stands draped in moonvine against the second retaining wall and is framed by a pair of tall Italian cypresses. On the terrace above, two dwarf weeping cherry trees thrive on either side while the third retaining wall, planted with more boxwoods grouped in threes, is visible. Pear trees are planted on the third terrace along with magnolias, which abound throughout the property. One of the first things Betty and Kendrick did was plant trees—about fifteen magnolias among other hardwoods and flowering trees. The land had to be totally cleared to create the terraces; the only trees that are original are the tall pines on the periphery of the property. The splendid home has settled in perfectly, surrounded with lush trees that appear as old and dignified as the house itself.

Immense, pink native azaleas frame the gazebo, which anchors the far end of the main courtyard garden where tulips and pansies abound in the annual spring beds.

One of a pair of putti stands on a stone capital behind the brick wall of the main courtyard garden.

A pretty yoshino cherry tree stands at the side of the front boxwood garden that encircles this stately fountain.

A tall pair of Italian cypresses frame the beautiful statue of Harvest that graces the retaining wall just beyond the courtyard garden.

A GARDEN TO LIVE IN

THE GARDEN OF
MR. AND MRS. PAT HOLDER

Pat and Barbara Holder have lived in their lovely home in
LaGrange since 1978. In that time, they have enhanced the house
dramatically and created the delightful garden from almost nothing.
Their home appears as a simple one-story, but the slope of the hill
provides the perfect spot for a large downstairs opening onto a
splendid rear garden. Edith Henderson originally planned a small
parterre for the home consisting of two circular beds of boxwoods
set directly outside the downstairs French doors. The backyard at
that time was mainly wooded, and the driveway came all the way
down and swung around in the back. Seven to eight years after they
moved in, the Holders cleared out the land and developed a long,
lush lawn that sweeps down to a tennis court partially hidden by
sweet autumn clematis and jasmine.

In 1998, Pat and Barbara hired architect Jack Jenkins to extend
the back of their house, creating a large living room surrounded by
tall French doors. On two sides, small iron balconies festoon the
French doors, while on the middle or back side, the doors open out

A beautiful wrought-iron bench is engulfed by ferns.

to a landing graced by a pair of grand brick stairs covered in fig vine. The spot that was created beneath this addition is a magnificent outdoor living area. The large brick columns that support the living room are swathed in climbing hydrangea, Confederate jasmine, and fig vine that has crept upon the ceiling. Algerian ivy, with its big, pretty, white-tipped leaves, wraps around the two front columns while a pair of consoles marks each wall and iron sconces create a magical light.

- Algerian ivy circles around the front columns of the outdoor living area, framing the view of the lawn.

- 'Zephyrine Drouhin' roses ramble up the curved iron railing while boxwoods anchor the base.

- 'Amethyst Falls' wisteria.

- A pretty stone flower basket marks the end of the hydrangea-lined path and the beginning of the boxwood-lined lawn.

- A charming cherub holds a pot of geraniums on his head in the bed bordering the patio.

- An inviting boxwood bench is tucked away along the hidden path that wraps around the side of the garden.

The old boxwoods from the original garden were preserved and moved to enhance the motor court in front.

Once this outdoor living room was created, the rest of the garden took shape. The Holders hired Brooks Garcia to plan the walls and beds on each side. The driveway was stopped short and a tall brick wall was built to enclose a patio where a large fountain against the far wall commands attention. The beds are delineated with rich, worn cobblestones that came from the old streets of downtown LaGrange. Barbara is a master gardener and has filled these beds with varieties of hydrangeas, camellias, azaleas, and a wide array of annuals. A beautiful boxwood hedge extends all the way around the elongated carpet of grass. Many of the boxwoods came from Pat's parents' home, Boxwood Acres in La Grange, where Pat grew up. They have also added many of the hardwoods to the property, including all of the magnolias, which mingle with the native dogwoods.

○● ○ 'Amethyst Falls' wisteria and
○ ○ 'Old Blush' roses climb the wall by
the pretty iron gate to the garden.

○○ ○ An antique urn holds fresh-cut
● ○ hydrangeas from the garden in
the outdoor living area.

○● ○ A statue of Pan hovers above
○ ○ the boxwoods along the lawn.

○○ ● Water lilies surround the stone
○ ○ frog in the koi pond.

○○ ○ A beautiful 'Perle d'Azur' clematis
○ ○ rambles around the iron form in
this antique urn, which is adorned
at its base with white snapdragons
and 'Iceberg' roses.

A WALLED GARDEN

THE GARDEN OF
MR. AND MRS. ZIM CAUBLE

Behind this stately Neel Reid–designed home in LaGrange is a beautiful, precisely manicured walled garden. Toni and Zim Cauble moved into this classic Georgian home in 1992 and have transformed the back gardens into a lush outdoor living space surrounded by rose borders whose enchanting scent fills the air. This home is unique in that the entire back is bounded by handsome old brick walls, some bathed in fig vine, others draped with clematis and others left to stand alone and serve as a backdrop to the gorgeous roses and flowering shrubs. Most of the hardscapes are original to the house, including the brick paths, patios, and the main brick walls; the gates and the far rear brick walls were added later. Brooks Garcia of Fine Gardens in Atlanta designed all of the current plantings, while designer Jeff Litrell added the stone features that accent the garden throughout.

The Cauble's elegant garden is approached from the side of the house where Brooks Garcia developed a street garden; visitors arrive and are greeted by lush plantings, which abound despite the tight space. Brick steps lead through a white picket gate to a sunken brick terrace to the right. Stone finials mark each stepped entrance, while tall Leyland cypresses delineate each corner. A low boxwood hedge borders the patio, with taller boxwoods serving as accents in each corner and at each turn. A wooden arbor drenched in climbing roses shades the entire area. These roses are not your typical climbers. 'Sombreuil' rose is an

A variety of roses fills the side raised beds of the main courtyard while a pair of stone finials marks the steps into the sunken terrace.

antique rose class "T" originating in 1850, and 'Buff Beauty' rose is a hybrid musk antique rose class "T" that originated in 1939. Toni explains that "Brooks suggested this retreat after a conversation about our love for dining alfresco, and the climbing roses offer the perfect coolness for spending many hours out here." A pretty iron chandelier planted with a maidenhair fern and fitted with candles hangs from the center of the arbor over a large dining table and chairs. A gorgeous pair of rusted floor lanterns further illuminates the intimate spot at night.

The brick path continues to a large patio centered at the back of the house, whose façade is even

more beautiful than the front. Graceful, circular steps lead down from the French doors and are framed by a lovely arch of climbing 'Sombreuil' roses anchored on either side in lattice stone planters. Directly on axis is a beautiful fountain attributed to Neel Reid centered on the middle of three arched walls bathed in fig vine. A lion's head spouts water into a large koi pond below. Two enormous boxwoods stand on either side with a climbing 'Sombreuil' rose in between that meanders up the wall to meet the tops of tall crepe myrtles from the other side. A lush lawn stretches out in front and is bordered by low brick walls on either side that hold raised beds planted with more roses. Some of Tony and Zim's favorite roses are 'Garden Party', 'Tiffany', 'Chicago Peace', 'Tropicana', 'Double Delight', and 'John F. Kennedy', many of which were suggested by Polly Mattox.

Beyond this center garden is the pool area, which is distinguished by a lovely, old wisteria arbor. Old lichen-covered chaise lounges and benches grace the edges while a variety of hydrangeas and rosemary spring up below. A pair of standard Pee Gee hydrangeas marks another white picket gate that leads to the rear walled garden. Here, more beautiful roses fill the low brick-edged borders. Clematis and climbing 'Buff Beauty' roses cover the white picket fence that borders one side. Besides all of these fabulous roses, Zim also grows lettuces and tomatoes in this rear garden. A stone obelisk dominates the garden, standing proudly at the center of the lawn while a pair of wooden lattice obelisks covered in vines gives height to the side borders and echoes the elegant centerpiece.

○ °° 'Sombreuil' roses climb the brick walls while 'Buff Beauty' roses climb the white picket fence in the rear garden.

○ °° The fig vine–covered fountain, attributed to Neel Reid, is framed by lush boxwoods and 'Sombreuil' roses.

○ °° A view across the courtyard lawn shows the sunken terrace shaded by 'Sombreuil' and 'Buff Beauty' roses that cover the arbor above.

○ °° A stately stone obelisk stands at the center of the rear garden while roses adorn the walls and fence.

○ °° 'Sombreuil' roses arch gracefully over the rear French doors of the Neel Reid home.

AN OLD GARDEN

THE GARDEN OF
MR. AND MRS. MADDEN HATCHER

Sally and Madden Hatcher moved back into her family's home in
Columbus in 1997. Sally lived here with her parents, the Bickerstaffs,
from the time she was thirteen years old and has many wonderful
memories of the home and her mother's garden. Thacker Cargill designed
the landscape for her parents, while landscape architect Hugh Dargan
has helped the Hatchers. Accenting the front façade, divided stairs are
enhanced with a small boxwood parterre planted with dazzling begonias
in the summer. 'Natchez' crepe myrtles frame the house and majestic oaks
dominate the front lawn across the circular drive.

The back is divided into three sections, the middle of which is
the main garden. Hugh Dargan added a pergola wrapped with radiant
'Lady Banks' roses and Confederate jasmine right outside the sunroom.
From here, the main garden presents itself. An extended rectangle, it is
centered on the home from the living room, whose great window seems
to bring the garden inside. A brick path leads along either side of this
garden to a brick patio the Hatchers added so that one may linger by the
fountain surrounded by lush azaleas and a cleyera hedge. The fountain

'Lady Banks' roses on the side pergola spill over the brick path leading
out to the left garden, where a spectacular viburnum blooms.

• ○ ○ ○
    ○   Ferns surround the pretty
fountain on the patio at the
far end of the main garden.

○ ○ • ○
    ○   'Perle d'Or' roses and pink
dianthus dazzle in the front of
the perennial bed of the main
garden while a sea of 'Rocket'
and 'Sonnet' snapdragons mix
in among the other flowers.

○ ○ ○ •
    ○   Caladiums proliferate under
the clipped sasanqua hedge
that defines the edge of the
left garden.

○ ○ ○ ○
    •   Fresh-cut tulips from the
garden adorn the table on the
side patio in the main garden.

creates a dramatic focal point against this far brick wall under the boughs of a stunning oak. On each side, white topiary camellias line the brick walls, with boxwoods planted in between and perennial beds in front. These camellias were planted by Sally's mom and are very old and grand; the exposed trunks are quite magnificent, covered in rich moss. A pair of exquisite vitex trees frames the house with a boxwood hedge stretching in between and Boston ivy clamoring up the brick around the large living room window.

To the left of the main garden, a pink sasanqua hedge, also planted by Sally's mother, is clipped in the same fashion as the camellias. It marks one side of another expanse of green lawn where a greenhouse covered in fig vine stores her orchids, among other plants. Large 'Tardiva' hydrangeas accent small paths hedged with mondo, while a variety of azaleas and hydrangeas proliferate. On the right side of the main garden, lustrous yoshino cherry trees and dogwoods prosper, their beautiful limbs filling the sky above the main garden's brick wall. Tulips abound here in the spring under the soft pink and white blooms. A verdant cluster of hydrangeas, including 'Annabelle', 'Snowflake', and 'Sister Teresa', takes over in the heat of the summer.

● ○ Boston ivy surrounds the living room window where
○ ○ boxwoods and tulips lie below. The pale pink of the
yoshino cherry trees from the side garden and the
white of the azaleas guide the eye beyond.

○ ○ A putti guards one of a pair of iron gates to the
● ○ main garden.

○ ● The beautiful blooms of yoshino cherry trees and
○ ○ dogwoods fill the air in the right garden while pink
tulips and azaleas abound below and the camellia
hedge of the main garden is visible just above.

○ ○ 'Rocket' snapdragons.
○ ●

BELLA FIORE

THE GARDEN OF
BETSY LEEBERN

A steep drive lined with beautiful, crisp maples leads up to the striking Italianesque home of Betsy and Don Leebern, "Bella Fiore," built in 1993 in Columbus. Perched at the top of twelve and a half acres, the formal gardens lay in terraces behind the grand home. Woodland trails lead all the way down to the base of the property, where a spectacular view back up to the house and its gardens captivates the eye, especially in early spring, when over 85,000 daffodils curtain the hill in a sea of yellow, white, and green. On the far wall of the elegant motor court, a splendid fountain is framed by lofty 'Natchez' crepe myrtles while boxwoods and asiatic jasmine soften the lines of the home. A wonderful patio off the right side of the house features an outdoor fireplace guarded by a bronze mountain lion that overlooks the side courtyard where ginger lilies and 'New Dawn' roses bloom amid dwarf Japanese maples and topiary waxleaf ligustrums. Boston ivy and fiveleaf akebia stream down the stairs leading to the pool and guest cottage where a vista opens over the hill. From here, the first long terrace begins back along the rear façade of the house.

A pair of 'Natchez' crepe myrtles frames the splendid fountain in the motor court.

Italian cypresses lend height to the long lawn, where perennial beds on either side are filled with spectacular peonies, hydrangeas, roses, and irises. Ilex hedges further define the space. On the fourth terrace, verdant ferns, hostas, and daylilies grow lavishly around a grotto draped with 'Lady Banks' roses where Poseidon reigns over the steep hill.

The woodland trails are on either side of the long, open slope; they include an azalea trail, a holly trail, and a hosta trail. Betsy has added the retaining walls and paths to help wind through the vast canopy of hardwoods. "I wanted to leave as much native as I could, but I wanted to be able to get through it," she explains. Some of the trees were cleared out, while others were put in, including over twenty beech trees, which hold their beautiful silvery leaves all winter long. The tulip poplar tree is Betsy's favorite; you will find an abundance of their magnificent, massive trunks.

○ ○ A sea of daffodils covers the hill up to the Italianate home.

● ○ Lofty 'Natchez' crepe myrtles frame the guest cottage.

○ ● The lush lawn of the main garden stretches out between the tall Italian cypresses in the perennial beds.

○ ○ A beautiful fountain draped in 'New Dawn' roses is the focal point of the courtyard by the side patio.

Native azaleas and oakleaf hydrangeas flourish among all of the striking buckeyes and rich ferns. Though a lot of the native plants were already here, they have been added to as well to enhance this naturalistic garden.

Betsy has made these woodland trails home to her grandchildren and to a host of animals. There is a picnic area and a playhouse tucked in by grand camellias, and several animal statues lend whimsy to the woodland scene, including a family of great bronze bears and a pair of deer that overlook the koi pond surrounded by rhododendrons at the base of a long, serene waterfall. Betsy is a true animal lover; a quaint bridge leads to her pet cemetery, and there is even a little fox den in her woods. They have had baby foxes two times. "They will come and sit on my back steps," Betsy notes.

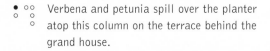 Verbena and petunia spill over the planter atop this column on the terrace behind the grand house.

Butterfly roses flourish behind a pair of stone columns and urns, which frame the entrance from the drive into the perennial garden.

'Festiva Maxima' peonies, bearded iris, and false indigo surround this putti in the main garden.

Poseidon reigns over the hill from his fabulous grotto.

A family of bronze bears plays among the woodland ferns.

A magnificent buck stands guard in the woods by the picnic area.

A GARDEN OF ROOMS

THE GARDEN OF SALLY FOLEY

For eighteen years, Sally Foley has lived in this splendid home on top of twelve acres of land that hold a series of beautiful gardens and grand vistas. Sally's father, Charlie Frank Williams, was in the concrete business and this was a small part of his Columbus rock quarry. Up the drive, past thickly planted azaleas and oakleaf hydrangeas, crepe myrtles, and stately magnolias, a grotto sits to the right, chiseled into a hill of stone where ferns have taken root. The front of the home is embellished with a small formal garden while a beautiful Perennial Garden lies just behind the home. A sequence unfolds from there, allowing panoramic views over the gently rolling hills where nineteenth-century Italian statues of each of the four seasons are placed strategically to captivate and focus the eye.

Three immense, striking holly obelisks mark the two tiers of the Perennial Garden. Roses climb up pretty iron forms, lending height along the beds, while perennials and annuals thrive below and soften the view over the expansive property. From here, steps lead down to a path through a curving boxwood hedge into the Rondele Garden where a pair

Roses climb up iron forms on both tiers of the Perennial Garden, where a beautiful view over the hill captivates the eye.

of gorgeous snowball viburnums mark the entrance. An enchanting fountain encircled by irises in the spring and cool caladiums in the summer stands at the center. A periphery of beautiful pink crepe myrtles encircles the entire garden. Another pair of snowball viburnums frames the entrance on the opposite side along with a pair of elegant benches.

The next garden in the sequence is the White Garden. Stone columns frame the entrance, which is reached through a graceful iron arch swathed in glorious

white wisteria and sweet autumn clematis. This short passage leads to the next garden, the Secret Garden, where an open lawn leads to two handsome flights of stairs accented by two pairs of urns planted with agaves. Lavish cryptomerias, 'Fosteri' hollies, and yews enclose the upper tier of the Secret Garden. A lustrous fountain boasts Poseidon at the center with Boston ivy and 'New Dawn' roses encroaching upon his face. The last garden—the Yellow Garden—winds back up the hill past a beautiful statue of Diana, the huntress, and on to the house, which sits atop the highest point of the property.

- Three immense 'Nellie R. Stevens' holly obelisks mark the steps beside the Perennial Garden and the path between the Rondele Garden and the house.

- An elegant pair of benches and a gorgeous pair of snowball viburnums mark the entrance into the Rondele Garden.

- Spring holds her head high among delicate flowering crab apples and grass that is blanketed in her season with golden daffodils.

- A lovely statue is draped by 'New Dawn' roses that grow all along the front façade of the home.

- Pretty stone finials mark one entrance into the garden where Boston ivy bathes the brick wall spilling over with 'New Dawn' roses.

A statue of Diana reigns over the Yellow Garden.

Urns planted with agaves flank the steps leading up to the fountain in the Secret Garden.

Italian cypresses planted in pairs interrupt the holly hedge by the pool, while white blooms of snowball viburnums are glimpsed beyond.

Yellow irises bloom beside the pool gazebo where a nymph draped with evergreen clematis supports the roof.

A mass of white roses leads into the Secret Garden.

A HISTORIC GARDEN

THE GARDEN OF
DR. AND MRS. PETER HOLLIDAY

The Hollidays' fabulous garden in Macon has been maturing and changing since 1854, when the house was built originally by the North family. Dr. and Mrs. Holliday and their children have lived here since 1984. Both Peter and Jeanne Holliday grew up in Macon and were familiar with the beautiful home and its spectacular garden, which is what really drew them to the property.

While the main garden is formal, meandering vines and shady retreats lend a softness that makes it very inviting. Though it was in great disrepair, the bones of the garden and most of the architectural elements that define the layout of the garden were already set in place when the Hollidays began working on it. They hired landscape architects Ryan Gainey and Macon native Alex Smith to help with the landscaping and design. James Farmer now oversees all of the beautiful plantings. What is so special here is that the integrity of the original garden has been upheld through the years as the visions of each owner not only have been respected but also have served as inspiration.

The Tinsleys bought the property from the Norths. In 1910, they added the top story, designed by Neel Reid, to the house and were the first

The iron gate, which leads from the side of the house
into the garden, was set in place by the Tinsleys.

From above, a grand cedar tree allows only half of the old boxwood parterre to be seen behind the original brick wall and gate.

Salvia and pinta fill the summer beds of the old boxwood parterre.

Beautiful spring tulips and pansies echo the curve of the staircase, whose columns are bathed in Confederate jasmine.

The staircase curves gracefully around each side of a mass of potted plumbago.

One of a pair of pretty stone fountains graces the walls of the pool house while an Italian cypress and geraniums fill a terracotta planter.

ones to actually cultivate a garden here. One of their biggest contributions was the long scuppernong arbor that defines the left side of the garden. Unfortunately, when the Hollidays bought the house, the arbor was totally dilapidated. They began restoring it immediately, and it is now completely refurbished and vibrant with scuppernong and 'New Dawn' roses.

A verdant width of grass stretches out from the arbor along the back of the house and is edged by massive azaleas in various shades of pink. The grass is bordered on the far side by a tall hedge with the first of three cherry trees filling in the corner. The Hollidays planted 'Lady Banks' roses, which grow densely and lavishly on both sides of the back of the house. The beautiful roses frame the loggia below the house, whose columns are entirely overrun by Confederate jasmine, whose white blossoms mix with those of the 'Lady Banks' roses for a splendid effect. A wrought-iron gate creates a focal point across the lawn at the center of the old brick wall wrapped in beautiful clematis separating this front garden from the formal boxwood garden beyond. Jeanne is careful to give credit to the gardeners of the past; many of the plants in this garden, like the clematis, have been here since the beginning. She calls

them "legacy plants": kerria, winter hazel, and a hedge of old-fashioned roses were all inherited. "They came with the house," says Jeanne.

The third owners, the Corns, bought the house in the 1930s. Pauline Pierce Corn—Polly—was an avid gardener; she even wrote a book about gardening, *Selections of Garden Ventures.* It was Polly who installed the stunning boxwood parterre that is the heart of the garden. The Hollidays added to the original boxwoods with others grown from clippings that Peter took as a child from a Monroe, Georgia, estate. In the center of the parterre is an enchanting fountain the Hollidays found in Morocco. It is encircled by myriad annuals, which create a canvas of colors within the low boxwood hedges; there are always flowers in bloom here. Taking advantage of Peter's love of hedging, Jeanne has him keep the boxwood garden in tip-top shape. "He's a surgeon, he likes to hedge," explains Jeanne. "He hedges everything in the garden." The Hollidays enhanced the far right side of the boxwood garden with a striking marble-and-iron gazebo they found at an auction. It is positioned beside the arbor and completes the vista from one end of the boxwood garden.

● ○ A beautiful marble-and-iron gazebo stands at the far side of the old boxwood parterre.

○ ○ An enchanting Moroccan fountain centers the old boxwood parterre where tulips and pansies flourish.

○ ● Pretty pots of rosemary and pink snapdragons flank the steps from the pool garden.

THE GARDEN OF POETRY AND PROSE

THE GARDEN OF
RYAN GAINEY

The extraordinary garden of famed landscape designer Ryan Gainey is tucked away on a secluded side street in Decatur. He bought the charming cottage in the early 1980s and has totally transformed the land and the neighboring property into a lavish series of outdoor rooms and a verdant maze of organized wilderness. His cottage is bathed in flowering vines, including the beautiful state flower, Cherokee rose, which envelops the entire side of his home. A pergola decorates the front and creates an intimate space overflowing with camellias, ferns, and roses. Around the side of the home, a pretty stone path leads beside a bed of overscaled fatsia and cast iron plant under an immense white oak on the right whose gracious boughs hold an elegant iron chandelier beckoning one through the rustic wooden gates beyond. "This garden is the story of my life," says Gainey. "Everything is integrated in my life."

A porch lined with salvaged columns looks out over stone steps packed with diverse planted pots onto a delightful stone terrace enclosed by stacked-stone walls. Beautiful beds overflow in front of the side walls while a dazzling koi pond lined with diminutive temples designed by Ryan fills the far right corner. A greenhouse patterned with diamonds of ivy on its panes fills the left corner. Ryan quotes one of his great teachers, Mr. F. W. Thode from Clemson University: "When you walk through the garden, the garden should walk with you." Curved stone steps lead under an extended arbor of rustic wood, which winds through the encroaching foliage of

Clipped ivy adorns the glass walls of one of the greenhouses,
where an iron palm designed by Ryan decorates the door.

massive rice paper plants, oakleaf hydrangeas, a variety of ferns, and countless other verdant greenery to a quaint guesthouse, a fabulous and intriguing tree house, another greenhouse, and a sunken toolshed. These riches abound under the canopy of a majestic deodar cedar and a gorgeous pair of massive dawn redwoods. "All of this is living walls, and the trees are the living ceiling," explains Ryan.

Returning to the walled terrace, splendid urns on the far left mark the path to the four garden rooms. Here, a hexagonal stone path culminates in a wooden pediment that leads to the neighboring vegetable garden. Along the way, garden rooms are laid out two on each side, directly on axis with each other. The first two approached are the Temple Garden and the Borders Garden. The Temple Garden overflows with an array of terracotta pots planted with various shapes of boxwoods, from balls, cones, and obelisks to topiaries, all centered by a fantastic iron gloriette over a stone-top table set on an embedded stone circle. A pair of charming wooden benches tucks in under the spilling foliage while espaliered pear trees line one side of the garden and espaliered apple trees line the opposite side, glorified in the center by a brilliant espaliered heart. The back of this garden is anchored by a magnificent wooden arbor graciously swathed in 'Amethyst Falls' wisteria, with columned apple trees dictating the front lines and a pair of grand crepe myrtles delineating the sides.

Dense Cherokee roses cover the side of Ryan's house.

A detail of the circular boxwood hedge in the Borders Garden shows the spikes of *Digitalis purpurea* 'Emerson' and *Dianthus barbatus* 'Newport Pink' engulfing the urn at its center and the lush blooms of 'Bobby James' roses on the wooden arbor.

Diminutive temples designed by Ryan line the koi pond while Macleaya grows up its stacked stone base on the walled terrace.

An old iron arbor frames the entry into the Oval Garden, where a *Hydrangea arborescens* 'Annabelle' blooms.

A pair of splendid urns planted with hostas stand atop the stacked stone wall of the terrace.

A wrought-iron chandelier hangs from the boughs of an immense white oak near the gates to Ryan's garden.

Directly across, steps lead down into the Borders Garden, where a series of three wooden posts with bent rebar wire creating an arch of 'New Dawn' roses marks each side of the central circular garden. Here, a circular planting of boxwoods frames a dramatic urn while stunning wooden arbors drenched in 'Bobby James' roses give height at each side. A low boxwood hedge lines the side beds where a whimsical topiary holly tree captures the eye on the right.

The gardens reached next along the path are the Oval Garden and the Arbors Garden. In the Oval Garden, a long green alley of lush grass contrasts with beds overflowing with hydrangeas, salvia, irises, roses, and 'Ryan Gainey' mums on each side and leads to the focal point: an old sundial that was part of Ryan's garden as a young boy. The Arbors Garden

In the Temple Garden, a poet's cupboard
upon the stone table holds a Ryan
Gainey poem reading,
"I gaze upon the garden
My heart grows peacefully still,
From its color comes my being
From its spirit comes my will."

A topiary holly tree captures the eye in
the Borders Garden.

Ryan designed this wonderful iron panel
of Adam and Eve to adorn the gate to
the Arbors Garden.

Wooden obelisks support tomato vines in
the Vegetable Garden.

- ○○ Three diamond boxwood
  parterres are the focus
  of the Arbors Garden,
  where lanterns hung from
  the rose-covered arbor
  highlight the pyramidal
  boxwoods at each center.

- ○ ●○ *Hydrangea arborescens*
  grandiflora 'Ryan Gainey'
  consumes the bed in
  front of this graceful
  architectural niche that
  holds a charming lead
  statue of Winter.

- ○ ○● 'Bobby James' roses
  cover one of a pair of
  wooden arbors that
  stand at each side of the
  circular boxwood hedge.

- ○ ○○ The boughs of a beautiful deodar cedar drape
  in front of the tree house.

consists of three magnificent diamond boxwood parterres
accented in the corners by raised squares and in the middle
by lofty pyramidal boxwoods. Rich camellias and ferns
flourish on the edges accented in different seasons by
purple poppies, daffodils, and foxgloves. An impressive
arbor densely bathed in lustrous roses covers the entire
garden while a series of three dazzling lanterns highlights
each diamond and creates a romantic and alluring feel.

AN INTIMATE GARDEN

THE GARDEN OF
MR. AND MRS. ALAN GREENBERG

From an exclusive Buckhead street in Atlanta, a pebbled drive winds up a steep hill. At the apex proudly stands the home of Joy and Alan Greenberg, designed by renowned architect Norman Askins and completed in 1988. Hugh Dargan designed the composed landscape to suit the home. Everything here was started anew; a former modern house was razed and the terraced yard was made into a grand lawn by creating stacked-stone retaining walls. Hugh Dargan explains, "The garden needed to be big and open, and simple, too," so as not to compete or conflict with the house. Everything is perfectly proportioned to suit the grandeur of the home. The front façade is embellished with a splendid motor court. To the right, parking is delineated by lustrous crab apple trees with ajuga below, while sycamores frame either side of the home and large, rich camellias lend height to the boxwood hedge along the façade. A hand-cut limestone path winds around the right side to the rear garden.

Hydrangeas, azaleas, and fatsia meld with annuals in deep beds on either side of the limestone path, which is carpeted between stones with

A statue surrounded by Chinese astilbe stands in the foreground by the arch leading into the Koi Garden.

dense mazus. The fatsia lends a warm, Mediterranean look, fitting to the Italianate home. This lushly enveloped path leads to a central terrace, which is embellished with an oval stonework pattern. Echoing the lines of the stonework, the front of the terrace curves out to meet the verdant lawn that stretches endlessly to magnificent gates. The Greenbergs found the gates and other ironworks that adorn the home on a buying trip in France with Norman Askins. The dramatic columns and iron gates appear to be the original entrance to the striking home, though they actually mark the rear of the property and enclose a small, hidden terrace. The long central lawn is flanked by boxwood hedges and intersects a perpendicular lawn at the far end, which opens out before the gates. Evergreens were added here on the periphery of the property, including lavish magnolias, cryptomerias, and spikes of lofty Italian cypresses. Pretty pink sasanquas are tucked in between and

lend soft color on a fall day to rival the vivid display of the hard-woods' brilliant oranges and yellows peeking from above.

On either side of the main lawn, the center of the boxwood hedges is marked by pairs of tall, conical boxwoods flanking limestone stairs. To the left is a pool whose graceful shape is repeated on the right by a refined koi pond. The Koi Garden is entered by these center stairs or at each end by an elegant iron arch swathed in vines. A beautiful fountain stands in the midst of the pool where dazzling koi whirl about in the dark water. Mondo surrounds the pool, whose limestone edge meets a scattered pebble path. Each end of the long garden is anchored by a lovely boxwood parterre where four boxwood beds embellished with seasonal flowers curve around a central ivy topiary. Four exquisite crab apple trees mark the far corners and reach out toward each other's beautiful boughs shading the garden below.

A beautiful overview of the Koi Garden shows the boxwood parterres planted with begonias that anchor each end.

Yoshino cherry trees line the steep drive.

Mondo borders the limestone coping of the koi pond.

A lovely statue is surrounded by Chinese astilbe at its base. Azaleas and oakleaf hydrangeas flourish behind.

A GARDEN FOR ALL SEASONS

THE GARDEN OF
MR. AND MRS. JOE WILEN

This beautiful Tudor-style home built in the twenties is tucked away in the woods off a pretty residential street in Atlanta. A long drive lined with yoshino cherry trees leads into a motor court defined by boxwood hedges and stacked stone walls with huge hydrangeas and azaleas spilling over the edge. The house is nestled off to the right. A grand oak with an old wooden swing dominates the front lawn while two graceful iron arches bathed in trumpet vine and jasmine mark woodland paths on either side of the lawn. A beautiful open gate to the left beckons one to discover the treasures of the gardens beyond.

The Wilens moved here in the late 1990s. They hired architect Yong Pak to renovate the house and hired landscape architect John Howard to lay out all of the hardscapes and the basic plan of the garden. Boxwoods Gardens has helped since then with the landscape design, changing out the flowers annually and tweaking things here and there so that through the years the garden has evolved into a gorgeous compilation.

There are two main gardens here with small gardens and paths interlaced throughout that connect the property. The front garden was originally the motor court. Now defined by tall brick walls and a magnificent iron gate built to replicate

Heavy with blooms, the boughs of the 'Natchez' crepe myrtles
spill over the boxwood parterre leading up to the house.

an old one from England, it has been transformed into a formal garden, very much the classic English garden. In the middle, a pretty fountain stands, encircled by a low boxwood hedge and verdant grass; the surrounding paths seem to form a perfect square. One side is defined by a handsome teak bench that is framed by a pair of lavish 'Tardiva' hydrangeas draping over pretty little statues. The remaining sides display a dazzling cascade of color in their beds while the far corner is marked by an inviting stone patio adorned with a variety of planters and charming iron chairs. From here, one may walk through the old conservatory doors of the breezeway to the main back garden or on through another door that leads to a manicured boxwood hedge, around and down stone steps through the center of a small rose garden to a pool area with a large terrace and cabana.

From the pool, an exquisite allée of standard-form 'Natchez' crepe myrtles frames a boxwood

A manicured boxwood hedge encircles the fountain in this classic English-style garden where foxgloves flourish in the spring beds.

Casa Blanca lilies spill over the boxwood hedge by a charming statue.

The fountain in this formal English-style garden is surrounded by a cascade of summer color.

Jasmine-bathed columns support the beautiful iron gate leading into the garden.

An array of pretty planters fills the corner of the stone patio.

parterre and softens the edges of the elegant yet strict lines of the Tudor home. Under the trees is a low boxwood hedge abounding with southern shield ferns and strawberry begonias; the backdrop is composed of sasanquas and hollies. Stone paths lead up on either side of the parterre to a pretty faux bois bench poised between stairs to the upper terrace. This center parterre is composed of three enormous boxwoods encircled with several rows of smaller boxwoods. Annual flowers create color in between while a series of conical boxwoods marks the edge. From the house, looking down the allée, the focal point is a pretty niche planted with cryptomerias framed by a pair of gorgeous viburnums. The cabana sits to the left so as not to impede the extraordinary view.

- A gorgeous boxwood parterre planted with 'Purple Wave' petunias completes this stunning allée of standard-form 'Natchez' crepe myrtles underplanted with southern shield ferns and strawberry begonias.

- Mountain laurel and rhododendron embellish the stone steps leading from the pool to the woodland paths.

- A spectacular jasmine-covered arch leads to a woodland path.

- An allée of 'Natchez' crepe myrtles softens the lines of the Tudor-style home.

- Spring flowers light up the beds by the iron gate of the English-style garden.

- 'Camelot' alba foxgloves highlight the boxwood parterre in the spring as the 'Natchez' crepe myrtles begin to leaf out.

THE BOXWOODS GARDEN

THE GARDEN OF
RANDY KORANDO & DAN BELMAN

Randy Korando and Dan Belman have lived in their Italianate home since the mid-1990s. They are the owners of the fabulous garden-and-home shop and landscaping team Boxwoods Gardens & Gifts in Atlanta. Together they had the vision to totally transform their house and surrounding land into the beautiful home and remarkable garden it is today. Finding a typical Georgian house from the 1940s, they added all of the stone elements, including an old balustrade, brackets, columns, and pediments. They also added a fantastic wrought-iron fanlight from the 1700s, which they found in Charleston, South Carolina. These antique pieces lend a unique character to the home. They grew dense ivy over the entire painted-brick façade, giving the appearance of old stone below. To complete the transformation, a dense hedge of 'Nellie R. Stevens' holly was planted as a front wall, with holly finials echoing the stone finials atop columns that anchor the stately iron gates.

The back of the home was completely wooded when Randy and Dan moved in. Being garden people, they set out immediately to create the lavish gardens and outdoor living space they so enjoy. The drive, which goes by the left side of the house from the large motor court, passes a lattice façade whose center pediment houses a lovely statue and whose sides and top are bathed in glorious 'Mozart' roses. Seasonal flowers are planted below. Randy designed the façade, along with most of the garden elements. Being a perfectionist like Dan, Randy likes to be hands-on and has also built many of the garden structures himself. Directly across the drive, Randy and Dan added a painted-brick wall to

Randy Korando designed the conservatory in the main garden.

enclose a small patio. Here, grand coral
azaleas create a dense interior wall while
a tall weeping cherry spills over the
thriving wisteria, which bathes the tops
of the brick wall and arches over the
iron gates marking the entrance.
They added a koi pond guarded by
iron herons and encompassed by a boxwood hedge. A great stone-top table
and old iron chairs complete the spot.

○ ●○ A handsome pair of faux bois benches
 ○ ○○ frames the entrance into the patio while
verdant wisteria swathes the top of the
painted brick wall and iron gates.

○ ●○ Stunning coral azaleas create a lush
 ○ ○○ background to the stone-top table and
old iron chairs near a small koi pond
guarded by iron herons.

○ ●● A sea of 'Snow' azaleas stand behind
 ○ ○○ this nineteenth-century carved stone
putti on the balustrade of the conservatory terrace.

○ ○● A gorgeous urn planted with caladiums
 ○ ○○ and petunias and encircled with old
Cherokee stones marks the entrance
into the main garden.

○ ○○ A stand of hemlocks provides the dense
 ○ ○● setting for the lattice façade draped with
'Mozart' roses and planted with 'Surfinia
Sky Blue' petunias and 'Babylon Light
Blue' verbena.

At the end of the drive is a gorgeous urn encircled by large Cherokee stones from the original front path of the house. A massive pair of windmill palms frames the entrance to the main garden where a turn-of-the-century zinc statue of a boy and a heron spouts water into the dark pool. Randy designed the divine pool and surrounding stonework, which radiates out at the far end and leads up to the magnificent conservatory. Lush lawn borders each side of the pool while swirls of boxwoods festoon the slope on both sides and Pee Gee hydrangeas flourish within the hedges. A smaller pair of windmill palms flanks the steps up to the terrace where a pair of nineteenth-century carved-stone putti stand atop a stone balustrade. The stucco façade of the conservatory is crisscrossed with ivy while glass doors lead into the haven made entirely from the original glass windows of the home's old sunroom. From here, a woodland path winds to an enchanting grotto. A statue rests upon a stone and dips his foot in the water that drips down from above. Autumn ferns and tassel ferns envelop the top and sides of the grotto while wild ginger and strawberry

The enchanting grotto made of stacked Cherokee stone is nestled in a mass of autumn ferns, tassel ferns, wild ginger, hostas, and strawberry begonias.

'New Dawn' roses ascend the side of the first small balcony and the large, top balcony.

An appealing putti.

Beautiful iron gates open onto the pebble drive leading to the Italianate home.

begonias adorn the front. The same woodland path continues around to another patio positioned just above the first and to a beautiful side entrance to the home. Here, Randy designed a tall, painted-brick wall elegantly arabesqued on top and strikingly fitted with mirrors within, creating another exceptional spot and providing privacy from the neighboring home.

'Snow' azaleas create a magnificent backdrop to the terrace of the conservatory, where one of a pair of nineteenth-century carved stone putti stands atop the stone balustrade.

Stone elements were added to the front entrance.

'New Dawn' roses climb up the wall in front of the open window on this top, back balcony.

Autumn ferns, hostas, and wild ginger proliferate along the woodland path beside this charming statue.

The tall and elegantly arabesqued brick wall is fitted with mirrors and adorned with ivy.

A ROSE GARDEN

THE GARDEN OF
MR. AND MRS. VERN DAVIS

Anna and Verne Davis moved to their home in Sandy Springs in 1995, intending to downsize from their former home in the Brookhaven area in Atlanta. The Davises have been working with landscape designer Brooks Garcia for years; he helped them re-create here the wonderful garden they had at their old home. They were going to simplify, but it just wasn't possible with Anna's insatiable love of flowers, particularly roses. The Davises had 350 roses in their old garden, and in about a third of the space they now have 150 roses, filling every nook and cranny of their new garden. "Brooks and I were very depressed leaving the old garden, so we got started right away," admits Anna.

Together they began on the garden before the house was even finished. The soil was very compacted, "the worst soil I have ever seen," says Anna. But they more than remedied the situation. They installed French drains to help and used yaupon hollies instead of boxwoods for all of the hedging; the hollies can tolerate more water. "There is limited space, so we have to garden vertically as well," Anna points out. A moon gate on the left of the house opens to a narrow corridor leading to the rear garden.

'Mozart' roses and 'Madame Isaac Pereire' roses intertwine with 'Sieboldii' clematis and 'Venosa Violacea' clematis on the moon gate leading into the garden.

Clematis twists about the moon gate while fig vine, Summer Wine roses, and 'Moonlight' Japanese hydrangea vine cling to the exterior brick wall of the home. Potato vine and Virginia creeper bathe the treillage installed on the opposite side.

The rear garden runs parallel to the back of the home, where benches set under a graceful arch dripping in hybrid musk roses anchor each end. A backdrop of hemlocks frames a fountain spilling into a koi pond planted with variegated iris, water lilies, duckweed, and parrot feather. On either side, flowers, shrubs, and an endless exhibit of roses abound. After they ran out of room in the ground,

Anna added twenty pots to her back deck and planted her more tender roses there. A horticulturist at heart, Anna has the names by all of her roses along with the date she planted them. She trained David Austin English Roses as climbers and they, along with 'Ballerina' roses and 'Eden' roses, bathe the back of their home, creating an extravagant display in the spring. This is Anna's third rose garden. Having learned the true colors, habits, and sizes of all of her roses, she knew precisely what would work with each other and where, and has thus created her perfect rose garden.

'Eden' roses and 'Ballerina' roses bathe the back of the house.

Streptocarpus blooms at the foot of this angel.

A pretty planter is filled with a variety of succulents.

Old columbine and a potted 'Nancy Jean' rose grace one entrance to the rose garden.

'Mrs. R. M. Finch' roses and Oriental poppies envelop the sundial on the left side of the path through the rose garden.

● ○ ○ Foxgloves abound under the cedar fencing of
○ the rose garden.

○ ○ ○ Yellow flag irises and water lilies fill the koi
● pond below the lovely statue of La Breeza, the
dancing girl.

○ ● ○ The large coral bloom of a 'Polka' rose intertwines
○ with the clusters of 'Pink Gruss an Aachen'
roses and 'Pat Austin' roses.

○ ○ ● 'Anna Rose Whitney' rhododendrons fill the
○ corner by one of a pair of benches that
anchors the far end of the narrow lawn
beyond the rose garden.

A RIVER GARDEN

A beautiful woodland property in Atlanta bordered on the
southeast side by a tributary of the Chattahoochee River is home
to a sprawling garden where three generations of a family live in a
compound of sorts. The original Greek Revival home built in the
thirties remains, though some of the property has since been divided.
However, the family bought twenty-three acres in 1997, comprising
the majority of the land. Architect Bill Harrison designed the main
house, which was completed in the winter of 2000; he also designed
the son's house. The daughter lives in the original home. There are
bike paths throughout the property for all of the grandchildren, as
well as a big central lawn and summerhouse where the family all
gathers on late afternoons.

The main house is situated on the crest of a hill with a view
stretching out from their back lawn down and across to a large pond,
which is home to a family of swans. Stone steps dotted with ground
cover and moss lead down beside a waterfall, past the White Garden
and on down to the fields. This whole lower area was wild with

The pond at the foot of the hill is home to a family of swans. A lush lawn stretches out from
here up to the main house, which is nestled among the hardwoods and surrounding gardens.

privet when the family arrived. Now, with the guidance of their good friend, landscape architect Jim Gibbs, it is perfectly manicured with a lush carpet of grass and hundreds of irises blooming around the pond in the spring and daylilies taking over in the summer. A picturesque bridge leads across the dark pond to a grass avenue situated under a canopy of hardwoods filled with a variety of hydrangeas, azaleas, dogwoods, and streams of more daylilies. There is a stone gazebo covered with roses at the end of the vista, and more roses climb along the handsome wrought-iron fence that borders the property at the crest of the riverbank.

- The stone gazebo is an inviting retreat at the end of the long grass path where daylilies provide a vibrant display.

- Daylilies abound in summer along the stream by the picturesque bridge.

- 'New Dawn' roses flourish along the arbor by the pool.

- An azalea blooms beside this stone bench by the koi pond.

- A dwarf Japanese maple and mountain laurel hide the arched stone bridge leading over the waterfall.

In contrast to the loose structure of the lower grounds by the river, a more formal perennial garden is situated toward the front of the property. A fountain stands by a pleasant seating area surrounded by a mass of annuals and perennials and marked by a set of five columns that line the back edge. A gracefully curved stone wall serves as a retaining wall on one side while spikes of flowers stand against its exposed side on the opposite end. A pair of elegant stone balls marks this entrance.

The stacked stone wall gracefully curves around the perennial garden.

The pale pink petals of penstemon blend with the hot pink blooms of lychnis.

Stepping-stones leading over the retaining wall mark the entrance on one end of the perennial garden.

Buttercup.

Stepping-stones softened by mazus lead through the perennial garden, where masses of buttercups, shasta daisies, and yarrow bloom in the spring.

A 1920s GARDEN

THE GARDEN OF
MR. AND MRS. EVERETT DOFFERMYRE

The Doffermyres have lived in their Georgian-style home in Atlanta since the late 1990s. Originally built in the twenties, it was designed by the architectural firm of Frazier and Bodin. It sits high atop a hill and is surrounded by massive old boxwoods, both English and American. Beautiful swooping hemlocks soften the lines of the house. Edith Henderson, a renowned Atlanta landscape architect, was the original designer and started these gardens early on, giving the whole property an established and romantic aura.

The Doffermyres asked Louise Poer to take control of the landscape design, and she has added to the main foundation of shrubs and trees. The driveway goes by the right side of the house past the huge boxwoods, on around to the back to a curved brick wall covered with dense climbing hydrangeas. From here, elegant stacked-stone steps ascend through gracious hemlocks to a small stone terrace. A tall iron urn on a pedestal spills over with flowers and marks the focal point, while a delicate iron chair on each side lends balance. The four corners are framed by more of the magnificent English boxwoods. From this landing, steps to the right lead up to the tennis court and steps to the left lead to a large stone patio and to the rest of the garden.

A mass of blue hydrangeas embellishes the side of this terrace
defined by stone steps and a white lattice obelisk.

The patio is long and narrow and serves as a border to the lawn. A gracefully curved pool surrounded by more stone lies parallel to the patio. Beyond the pool, the lawn is lined with huge hydrangeas and camellias that lead up the hill to the cabana. The lawn is broken into two long terraces, each marked by extended stone steps. The first set of steps is flanked by a pair of terracotta urns; the second set is flanked by white lattice obelisks. The last terrace is enclosed with a curved brick wall that is festooned with deep swags of ivy. In the center, a lovely statue surrounded by hollies and hostas stands at the foot of the cabana stairs.

The 1920s Georgian-style home is surrounded by massive boxwoods.

Blue hydrangeas stand out among the dense green of old boxwoods and immense camellias by the pool.

Lustrous 'Pink Perfection' camellias and boxwoods divide the pool garden and the formal garden.

Stacked-stone steps surrounded by swooping boughs of hemlocks lead to the garden.

Majestic 'Pink Perfection' camellias illuminate the formal garden in the winter.

Evergreen clematis covers the roof of this potting shed at one end of the formal garden.

'Iceberg' roses and bearded irises thrive in the spring beds of the formal garden.

Ground orchids.

An old urn in the pool cabana is filled with fresh-cut hydrangeas from the garden.

Clipped ivy decorates the old brick retaining wall while potted begonias frame the lovely fountain in the formal garden.

Squeezing through a path framed by more exquisite boxwoods, one reaches a small formal garden. The central path is marked by robust boxwoods whose height has been checked so as not to spoil the view of the formal beds. A potting shed covered with evergreen clematis mirrors the house, complete with slate roof, and anchors one end of this formal garden. Directly across stands an old brick retaining wall with a fountain on axis. This formal garden is broken into four rectangles framed by L-shaped beds all separated by brick paths bordered with mondo. Anemone, phlox, iris, ground orchids, peonies, and roses are a few of the flowers gracing the beds. 'Pink Perfection' camellias planted on one side tower over the formal garden, creating a dense hedge that separates it from the pool garden.

A FORMAL
GARDEN

THE GARDEN OF
MR. AND MRS. TED PLOMGREN

Ted and Pat Plomgren's garden is both sophisticated and quaint, which makes for an almost casual elegance. Nestled into an idyllic Vinings neighborhood in Atlanta, this relatively small piece of land abounds with radiant color bursting through the dense, lush green, which frames the charming architecture of the garden. "We have used every inch," says Pat, but they have used restraint as well. There is a controlled element here; careful artistic composition assures that not too much is exposed in any one view.

There are two terraces that immediately help define smaller vistas and add an element of surprise: the second terrace is entirely out of view until you reach the edge of the first. Each is harmoniously proportioned with repeating architectural elements that seem to unite the rich, overflowing garden. A natural rhythm is created with complementary colors and recurring flowers dotted throughout, and this ensures a seamless flow between the different areas so the eye is not distracted by the abundance but pleased by the overall effect.

The Plomgrens have been here for twenty-three years, but work on the garden didn't begin until 1988. Ted saw landscape architect Dan Franklin's

'Fortune's Double Yellow' roses cover the roof of the greenhouse
while sprays of 'Snowmound' spirea cascade around the fountain.

garden on the cover of *Southern Living* and was immediately struck. He called Dan and said, "I want a garden like yours." The Plomgrens' backyard was originally very sloped. The first thing Dan did was create the two terraces and connect the separate areas with handsome stone steps. They also immediately upgraded the soil. "It's all about good dirt," says Pat. "Every one of these beds has been dug up about eighteen inches and filled in with good dirt. One anniversary my husband and I even gave each other a truck full of dirt." The Plomgrens developed a special formula with Dan. The result is this extra-rich soil that produces the extraordinary, verdant vegetation.

The upper terrace is dominated by a center medallion boxwood parterre that is anchored by a Chinese evergreen oak. To the left of the medallion is a beautiful old greenhouse that has weathered to a worn red. Ted and Pat discovered it at the New York flower show; a man from Virginia was using it as part of his display. The Plomgrens fell in love with its old-world charm and knew exactly where it would go in their garden. They bought it on the spot and had it shipped in pieces to Atlanta. They then doubled its size. They added a mirror image to create the pleasing "U" shape that seems to embrace the left side of the garden and harbor the fountain at its center front. Vines bathe the outside while potted begonias overflow out the open windows and beckon one inside, where more plants abound.

To the right of the center medallion is a potting shed Pat designed herself, complete with nineteenth-century shutters she found in Connecticut. The bed in front of the potting shed repeats the same elegant curve as the bed in front of the greenhouse. A magnificent obelisk has been added here and is surrounded by irises in the spring and hydrangeas in the summer.

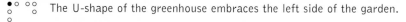

The U-shape of the greenhouse embraces the left side of the garden.

A boxwood hedge curves out to encompass the obelisk surrounded by a variety of hydrangeas.

A pretty iris blooms in the bed in front of the rustic wooden fence at the edge of the upper terrace.

Potted begonias highlight a lantern on the ledge just inside the greenhouse.

The boxwood hedges lining the stone path to the gazebo curve around to encircle the separate gardens on the lower terrace.

The 'Paula Fay' peony is an early bloomer.

A fountain is enhanced by lush boxwoods in front of a twig façade.

A rustic wooden fence covered in roses borders the edge of the upper terrace. From here, graceful steps lead down to the more formal lower garden. To the immediate left and right of the stairs there are rose beds tucked behind low boxwood hedges. The climbing roses from the wooden fence above hang down, connecting the two terraces. A stone path on axis with the stairs leads to a twig gazebo dripping with more flowering vines. This path is delineated by a boxwood hedge that borders the stone path and then curves back to encircle the separate gardens on each side. The right garden is a boxwood parterre filled with gorgeous 'Paula Fay' peonies, behind which stands a detailed twig façade with a patterned pediment that creates a striking backdrop to the lovely fountain. The same pediment is repeated on the arbor directly across in the left garden, with hydrangeas on either side encroaching upon a small fountain. A checkerboard lawn of limestone and grass stands out in front with a lone antique ball at its center.

○ ● Dazzling 'Paula Fay' peonies fill the boxwood parterre on the lower terrace.

● ○ 'Paula Fay' peony.

○ ● A striking checkerboard lawn of limestone and grass is centered by a lone antique ball on the lower terrace.

○ ● The pediment of this twig arbor repeats the pediment of the twig façade in the boxwood parterre directly across.

A GARDEN SURPRISE

THE GARDEN OF
MR. AND MRS. HERNDON MURRAY

Behind this timeless Tudor-style home in Atlanta lies a most magnificent and unexpected garden. Herndon and Wendy Murray moved here in the late 1980s and developed the naturalistic and majestic garden that is here today. The English cottage–style home was built in 1934 by noted architect James Wise. What is so marvelous is the property itself: it is an old rock quarry, originally mined during the Civil War and then again in the early twentieth century to excavate the stone for the curbs when this neighborhood was developed.

The Murrays added the pretty window boxes and the trellises, which are bathed in blossoming vines; they "tried to make it into a garden house," Wendy says. The architecture dictates this as well with rooms that get deeper and deeper so that everything opens onto the garden. On the front left of the house, the Murrays added a spectacular rose garden set in a circular boxwood parterre divided into four sections. The strict balance of this front rose parterre stands in striking contrast to the creative disarray of the back garden. A pretty brick path leads through the roses under a wooden pediment that matches the pediment adorning one of the front windows, also covered in climbing roses.

A mossy path among the lush ferns and thick hydrangeas
leads to this quaint bridge over a trickling stream.

This dramatic rear garden is filled with verdant vegetation: massive hydrangeas, azaleas, and a variety of native plants flourish in the moist atmosphere. Everything here is very rich; there is "beautiful, beautiful soil because of all the rocks," explains Wendy. Volunteer impatiens run wild and fill every crevice of the cool stone walls with a vivid display of color, all the way to the top height. A natural waterfall at the back of the property creates a serene spot after a heavy rain. Trickling into a clear pond below, it continues as a stream along the right side of the lawn. "I tried to work with what would work here, in this environment, which is more like the mountains," Wendy explains. "I used native plants, rhododendrons, laurels, and ferns, native perennials that would proliferate and spread because I just didn't think everything should be lined up."

⠏ The rose garden completes the English cottage feel of the 1934 Tudor-style home.

⠗ The rose-covered pediment leads from the front rose garden to the garden behind the house.

⠎ The rose garden is set in a circular boxwood parterre.

⠑ Stepping-stones curve around the left side of the garden by caladiums and a variety of hydrangeas.

⠞ Ferns engulf this quaint statue.

⠋ A wooden pediment drenched in climbing roses adorns one of the front windows.

⠛ The pretty stone retaining wall behind the rose garden is decorated with arches of climbing roses.

⠓ The soaring granite walls of the old quarry are visible behind oakleaf hydrangeas.

⠚ The scale of the bench in front of the pool retaining wall shows the vastness of the old quarry walls.

AN UNEXPECTED SPLENDOR

Along a prestigious street in the Buckhead area of Atlanta lies a stunning garden hidden from passersby by dense plantings along the periphery. The elegant brick home is approached by a curved drive lined with lush trees and massive azaleas. The home itself is bordered with manicured boxwoods while a pair of immense Japanese maples softens the wings and frames the original structure. These gardens were begun in 1997, but the owners have lived here almost thirty years; for a while they only gardened at their farm. However, the gardens seem as old as the grand home itself. Beginning big and with fervor, the owners added over four hundred sizable trees, as well as numerous shrubs and flowers, lending a feel of luxuriant abundance.

A waterfall can be heard to the right, where fantastic hemlocks and other hardwoods frame a path leading into the woodland trails. Large stepping-stones lead back and forth over waterfalls and a creek brimming with trout and bass. The air is cool and misty, and a variety of ferns, sasanquas, azaleas, and oakleaf hydrangeas encroach upon each step beneath the thick canopy. An azalea and dogwood trail opens up and the creek gracefully falls down to a vast, dark pond densely planted with hostas. A glimpse back up offers a view of the back corner of the house over a sea of roses to a beautiful stone terrace crowned by the elegant balustrade of a balcony above.

This first pond cascades down to two smaller ponds where, finally, a lawn stretches out on either side. Backed by hemlocks and Leyland cypresses, the lawn highlights a colossal hill of fabulous azaleas, which appears as a glorious and dramatic azalea bowl. The rose garden is next. A charming white picket fence embellished with clusters of 'Ballerina' roses encloses the entire garden while beautiful rose arbors mark the entrances. A fountain stands at the center of the

The pool gazebo bathed in 'Blaze' roses and embellished with Knockout roses below is reflected in the dark water of the still pond.

Clipped ivy covers the façade of the timeless home while 'New Dawn' roses wrap around a tall pine.

Autumn ferns encroach upon the edge of the back waterfall.

The soft blooms of strawberry begonias highlight the side of the waterfall.

Long stills of roses and vegetables abound in the rose garden while clusters of 'Ballerina' roses adorn the white picket fence and 'New Dawn' roses cover the small arbor.

profuse and precise rows of roses and vegetables. "I have fond memories of the time I spent at my grandmother's house while growing up," the owner says. "She always had roses and was always working in her rose beds." A garden house bathed in 'Blaze' roses and framed by magnificent magnolias anchors the back of the broad garden. Stacked-stone steps on axis with the fountain and the garden house lead through an iron arch flanked by more rich magnolias to the verdant lawn that stretches out behind the home. Voluminous perennial beds spill over the graceful curves of the bluestone border. The long lawn leads to a short path that cuts back

to the stairs leading up to the pool area, where a pair of exquisite crepe myrtles swathed in 'New Dawn' roses frames the gates. Roses and Boston ivy lavishly bathe the back of the extraordinary home. Roses are a constant here. "I plant roses that I like in the next available space; there is no rhyme or reason," says the owner. Hidden wires between columns at the back of the home are cleverly entwined with lines of alluring 'Blaze' roses, creating a most spectacular effect. More of the 'Blaze' roses climb up the gazebo at the far side of the dark pool and the cabana.

A small walled garden adjacent to the right of the back façade of the home makes a lasting impression. Overhung by a graceful stone balustrade festooned with 'Felicia' roses that continue up the columns, a striking statue stands at the center pouring water from her jug into the low basin. More roses abound in the perimeter beds behind boxwood hedges while climbing hydrangea, fig vine, roses, and wisteria envelop the side walls, creating an enchanting, secluded feel.

• ○○ Exquisite hemlocks provide a lush backdrop to the bed of roses in the pool garden, where a bronze statue stands on the balustrade beyond.

○ ○○ A splendid terracotta urn planted
• with striking red flowers sits atop a pedestal in the perennial garden among the dense hemlocks.

○ ●○ A striking statue stands at the
○ center of the walled garden while a perimeter of rose beds gives way to 'Felicia' roses climbing up the balustrade and columns.

○ ○● 'Blaze' roses create a wall of deep
○ pink blooms in between columns by the pool garden.

Knockout roses line the side path from the perennial garden to the pool garden.

An arch through the magnolias leads to the rose garden.

Voluminous clusters of 'Ballerina' roses decorate the white picket fence surrounding the rose garden while 'New Dawn' roses bathe the arbor.

The pleasing form of the pool gazebo covered in 'Blaze' roses is reflected in the dark pool.

A CLASSICAL GARDEN

THE GARDEN OF
DR. AND MRS. ROBERT GILBERT

This historic garden in Atlanta was originally designed in 1928 by famed landscape architect Robert Cridland. In 1985, Dr. Robert and Joan Gilbert moved into the beautiful, Georgian-style house designed by architect Philip Thornton Marye. The old gardens were completely overgrown when the Gilberts first bought the house, but they are what initially attracted Bob, and he immediately set out to restore them to their former glory. "We tried to leave as much as we could" of the original gardens, says Bob.

Grand boxwoods wind about a stone stepping path that unexpectedly opens onto a magnificent statue of Summer encircled by the old, voluptuous boxwoods set above low stone walls that define the circular garden. A pair of curved stone benches further glorifies the hidden niche. On axis with Summer, stone steps descend a set of three terraces and culminate in another small, circular garden where a koi pond is marked by a pretty stone fountain accented with a large, irregular stone border and softened with mondo. The view back up to Summer from here is quite breathtaking through the rich boxwoods, which are bordered by tall magnolias and beautiful hemlocks whose limbs feather around Summer's striking figure.

Boxwoods encroach upon the stone steps leading
up to the magnificent statue of Summer.

The stone steps continue down to a beautiful, sunken boxwood parterre. On the first landing overlooking the parterre, a smaller statue holding a lantern beckons you forward under the heavy boughs of a magnolia, down the remaining flight of steps into the White Garden. This garden was created and designed by Bob with the help of Jeremy Smearman from Planters. The refined pattern consists of a central circular garden of boxwoods dominated by a handsome statue surrounded by foxgloves, irises, and allium and planted with topiary camellias, spikes of yews, and 'Sister Teresa' hydrangeas in the four corners. A central path leads out to the side rectangular gardens, which echo one another in design with a large, middle boxwood enclosed by a hedge of lower boxwoods with tufts of exquisite gardenias springing up within each corner. The outer beds are planted with more dazzling touches of white blooms of hydrangeas, camellias, and annuals among the lush green boxwoods.

- Old boxwoods set above low stone walls encircle the statue of Summer.

- The three parterres of the White Garden are just visible from this viewpoint.

- Tall spikes of phlox surround this handsome statue in the center parterre of the White Garden.

- Coming down the steps towards the White Garden, boughs of a magnolia frame the first boxwood parterre.

AN ENCHANTING FRENCH GARDEN

THE GARDEN OF
ELIZABETH HOLT

In 1994, Elizabeth Holt moved into her English cottage–style home tucked away in a quiet neighborhood in Atlanta. The gorgeous plantings around the mailbox hint at the treasures beyond. Elizabeth hired landscape architect Bill Smith to help with the design in 1995, and the two have been reinventing and enhancing the garden ever since. They created a small perennial garden to the left where the parking once had been. "I have a thing about birds and flowers," remarks Elizabeth. This little U-shaped garden is flanked by a pair of small cherub statues at the front and is accented by an old wellhead at the top. From here, five French buhr stones carpeted with bluestar creeper within and pebbles between create a path leading beside the house to the garden beyond. A boxwood hedge marked by a pair of obelisk boxwoods leads to a small walled garden where stone flame finials stand at each corner column. 'Iceberg' roses wrap around the curved brick wall and continue climbing up onto the house. A sundial sits beneath the bay window and is framed by a pair of standard Pee Gee hydrangeas.

A herringbone brick path continues from here by a glorious, curved wall bathed in dense sasanquas with an unusual chain-link boxwood parterre

'Foxy' foxgloves overwhelm the terraces
leading up to the summerhouse.

below. Another small pair of cherubs sits at the base of brick steps that lead through a series of iron arches steeped in vines to create a loggia wrapping around the left side of the main garden. Formerly just a simple brick patio with grass stretching to the brick retaining wall, this garden has been transformed into an overwhelming sea of flowers. Elizabeth and Bill cleared the ivy and 'Bradford' pears, which were the only plantings beyond the retaining wall. They created three terraces with brick steps leading up the center to a summerhouse designed by Bill Smith. Here, an enchanting statue of Diana stands guard over

•○ ○ Tall spikes of foxgloves define the edge of the first terrace of the main garden in late spring.

○• ○ A variety of delicate tulips overflow along the first terrace in the main garden in early spring.

○○ • Stunning 'Delaware Valley' white azaleas frame the French blue summerhouse in the main garden where an array of tulips abound.

○○ ○ 'Lady Banks' roses hang over the beautiful nineteenth-century French fountain of the koi pond.

the garden. Planter boxes with tall, conical box-woods mark two terraces where stone paths curve out from each side along flower beds as vivid colors proliferate and dazzle the eye. The French blue summerhouse tops the final terrace, echoing the blue of the planter boxes. This summerhouse was completed in early 2000 and makes a stunning focal point for the garden framed by a pair of enormous 'Natchez' crepe myrtles. To the left, the curved loggia beckons you under its arches, where ferns, creeping jenny, ajuga, and hostas crowd around stepping-stones. To the right, a woodland path leads around massive azaleas and hydrangeas planted among the trees.

On the other side of the curved patio, 'Lady Banks' roses filter over an elegant stone fountain, which spouts water into a basin swimming with koi and flanked by topiary ball boxwoods. A pretty cherry tree arches over an iron arbor rich with green foliage near tall brick walls curtained in fig vine and 'Mermaid' roses. Continuing around to the front of the house, a secret spot is off to the left, nestled under the draping boughs of maples and cherries. A fantastic bench designed by Bill rests here alluringly in the shade among the ferns; this is one of Elizabeth's favorite spots.

•○ ○○ Two pairs of French blue
 ○   planter boxes mark the terraces
        of the main garden steeped
        with tulips and other early
        spring flowers.

○● ○○ Stepping-stone paths thick
 ○   with spring color curve out
        from the brick steps leading
        up to the summerhouse.

○○ ●○ Sunlight filters through the
 ○   limbs of a kwanzan cherry and
        a pink native azalea above a
        lovely bench designed by Bill
        Smith, which is nestled among
        hellebores and blue scillas.

○○ ○● The three tiers of the main
 ○   garden display a gorgeous
        array of tulips and other
        early spring flowers.

○○ ○○ 'Angelique' and 'Mount Tacoma'
 ●   tulips spring up among daffodils
        and violas on the brick path
        leading through the breezeway,
        framed by a pair of Regency
        pedestals and potted white
        impatiens.

A GARDEN WITH A VIEW

THE GARDEN OF
MR. AND MRS. CHARLES SHAW

This extraordinary mountain garden in Rome is a cool and inviting retreat steeped in verdant greenery and a wild display of color. Marion Shaw and her husband, Charles, have lived here for twenty years. In that time, they have completely transformed the house and the surrounding land. The Shaws were living in a restored Victorian in downtown Rome when Charles first drove Marion up Mount Alta to see this site. "At first, I wouldn't get out of the car," says Marion, recalling that the house looked more like a ranch-style motel—long and low, with a mansard roof—than a house. What's more, "there wasn't a single shrub on the property." But when she walked around the back of the house and took in the stunning view, she had an abrupt change of heart. Today, a wonderfully charming cottage sits tucked away among the lush vegetation and fresh mountain air.

Native and kousa dogwoods define the front of the property along with enormous hydrangeas. A graceful stacked-stone wall curves artistically along the left of the lawn. A very hands-on

The stunning mountain view is highlighted by 'Annabelle' and 'Nikko Blue' hydrangeas.

gardener, Marion created and built this wall herself, building on the former simple railroad ties, which were a bit severe. Irises, phlox, ferns, oakleaf and double hydrangeas, soapwort, and tall spikes of hollyhock spill over the wall. More varieties of mophead and lacecap hydrangeas are dotted throughout. An enchanting 'Moonlight' Japanese hydrangea vine bathes the trunk of a tall pine tucked behind all of this color.

A variety of blue lacecap and mophead hydrangeas fill the space under these dogwoods defining the left side of the drive. Climbing hydrangea bathes the corner of the charming cottage while Boston ivy covers the chimney.

Balloon flower and soapwort cascade over this stacked-stone wall designed and built by Marion herself.

Blue lacecap hydrangea, ferns, and dusty miller are among the many lush plants in the raised bed that curves around the side of the house.

A stacked-stone wall spills over with soapwort among other perennials and hydrangeas as it gracefully curves around the corner of the house, which is softened by more of the massive hydrangeas.

'Moonlight' Japanese hydrangea vine winds up the pine tree situated among hydrangeas, providing a lush backdrop to Marion's hydrangea cuttings.

Marion adores all plants in and of themselves, and she seems to be a true botanist at heart. Though she is not technically a master gardener, she knows all of her plants by their botanical names. She even propagates her own hydrangeas. Every late July, when the stems get woody, Marion takes cuttings of all her different varieties and roots them. She has a whole system on the left side of the house, an outdoor greenhouse of sorts, with all of her baby hydrangeas. "I root all of these, I take cuttings; I just like to do that. It's fun," she says. Among her different hydrangeas is the variety 'Beni Gaku' from Seattle. The bloom "is first a delicate pink, then blue, then in the fall it turns red." She also has 'Madame Emile Mouillère', 'Blueboy', 'Annabelle', 'Snow Flake', and 'Nikko Blue'. Everything here seems to thrive under Marion's care. She has made this land into a delightful, almost magical home overflowing with superb blooms and rich flora.

°° ° Virginia creeper and a wrought-iron lantern frame this magnificent mountain view from the Shaws' porch.

°° ° Blue lacecap and mophead hydrangeas fill the space under these dogwoods enclosing the front lawn.

°• ° Japanese iris 'Royal Robe'.

°° • An array of hydrangeas abounds on this mountain property.